The State of

California

Growing Up

Foreign in

the Backyards

of Eden

Ted Pejovich

ALFRED A. KNOPF   NEW YORK   1989

The State of

California

THIS IS A BORZOI BOOK
PUBLISHED BY ALFRED A. KNOPF, INC.

Portions of this book have appeared in *The Quarterly* and in *StoryQuarterly*.
Grateful acknowledgment is made to New Directions Publishing
Corporation and Faber and Faber Limited for permission to reprint
an excerpt from *Canto XIII* from *The Cantos of Ezra Pound* by Ezra Pound.
Copyright 1934 by Ezra Pound. Reprinted by permission of New
Directions Publishing Corporation and Faber and Faber Limited.

Library of Congress Cataloging-in-Publication Data
Pejovich, Ted.
The state of California.
1. Pejovich, Ted—Childhood and youth.   2. Children
of immigrants—California—Biography.   3. California—
Biography.   4. Poor children—California—Biography.
5. California—Social life and customs.   I. Title.
CT275.P535A3   1989   979.4 [B]   88–45489
ISBN 0-394-56863-X

Manufactured in the United States of America
First Edition

For the family Pejovich,
for Anne,
and for Gordon Lish

And Kung said, and wrote on the bo leaves:

     If a man have not order within him

He can not spread order about him;

And if a man have not order within him

His family will not act with due order;

     And if the prince have not order within him

He can not put order in his dominions.

         —Ezra Pound, *Canto XIII*

My father was buried holding his hat to his chest, the black-banded, crimson-topped pillbox cap of the national costume of Montenegro, where he was born in whatever year just before 1900 that my father needed to write on the piece of paper in order for him to get a passport. My father wore a beret in France, a miner's hard hat in Canada, and a soft felt fedora or a creased Panama in California, the state we both adopted, he as a father of four, and myself as the youngest and the only son, the bearer of the name, in those spare years just after the war when California was getting ready to be golden again.

Montenegro is a high and rocky place and the plots of land in the mountains are small. The idea was always to go to a place where money could be earned and sent back to buy enough land to feed more than just the cow and the goat and to keep shoes on everybody's feet. My father left his homeland at twenty and came back some forty years later with his American passport strapped in a canvas wallet around his waist.

The old Montenegrins call their homeland "Dear Sister" and my father always thought of himself as one of her brothers, never really so far away, but he came home from that trip and said that whatever Eden he had was right here underfoot, in this hard garden they called America, where he had earned his bread and raised his children and where he would be put into the ground.

My father is buried at the Serbian Orthodox Cemetery in Colma, California, a narrow fertile valley just south of San Francisco where flowers are grown in fields and under chalky glass greenhouses for the corner flower stalls of the city.

This book is a meditation on the lives of those of my family who left their homeland and who lived their lives everywhere else thenceforward as strangers; on that childhood with sisters when I was the incense-bearing witness to christenings, communions, marriages, burials and wakes—the dreams I dreamed in my father's hat, out in that garden that was California in the fifties, and in that golden sun.

[T.P.]

The State of

California

Points of Interest

Ⅰn the square, in front of the
People's Cafe, my wife says that we have to get on the road
and find this place while the sun is still on our side, before we
have to race the sun back down to civilization, to water and
to beach, and to one of those at least decent little cafes full
of Germans with air mattresses and Italians with kids, and
to our room in the long stone house run by the squat man in
suspenders who had said that he had cut every stone of the
house himself, cut every square corner of every last block
with his own hands, the way the man had said he had cut
seven years of new stones for the fortress of Sveti Stefan be-

low, sticking out into the water like a stone fist, the man in the suspenders had said, find this place before we have to race back down the mountain to our room in the house on the hillside where the sign at the end of the driveway says it in all of the four languages on all of the menus around here, the sign you can see up in a window or stuck down off the road in front of most of the houses that are a stone's throw up the hill from the water, the sand, and the rock monastery made over into a hotel, walled up out there against God and the tide just two strokes shy of sin, the man in the suspenders had said, the sign that says: SOBE ZIMMER ROOMS CAMERE, stuck down at the end of the dirt driveway where the guests' cars are parked in jags along the side of the hill, and where the man in suspenders puts a stone behind a back wheel and says it is so that you will not have to go looking in the morning in all of that crystal blue down there for what the fish cannot stomach—a couple of rubber tires and that hunk of god-forsaken tin sunk into the sand under their sun-spoiled heads.

What we are looking for now is a place to throw away the meat that the waiter brought back wrapped in white paper, a trash can or a barrel to drop this in to get rid of the smell, but my wife and I do not see any trash cans at corners or any sort of waste basket near the yellow stone building we had walked through before lunch to see how the king had lived. What we see are streets without sidewalks, walking one block

4

and then another, looking for a garbage can or for one of those wire mesh baskets that you might find in a park, and what I see first, and then what my wife sees is something in a driveway I know is more than a dog sleeping, or less than a dog sleeping, with flies all over the side of it on the bare parts and on the fur, and my wife says to go ahead and just throw the packet anywhere so that we can get out of this place where a king could have lived once and a dog today cannot, but I say that we can throw the packet away someplace else, out of town where no one can see us throwing food away in the street, and we hurry past the woman pouring milky water out of a bucket into the gutter in front of her house to the car parked under trees near the yellow building that is the palace, and grind gravel out of the place that we only have the little street map for, the map from the travel office that has the points of interest starred and arrows darting the main road at opposite ends, the one arrow pointing toward Titograd and the other arrow pointing back the way we had come, toward Sveti Stefan and the ocean down below, and we turn sharp and trail the arrow vectored inland from the coast and dart off the paper farther along, somewhere into brush, granite and sky, with the packet of wrapped meat sitting on the dashboard and the windows rolled all the way down, and my wife says that we are going to swim all day tomorrow for certain, all day in the blue, blue, blue of the sea.

. . .

5

My wife says to please throw the packet of meat out, to just toss it out of the window, but I say we should wait until we are off of the asphalt and away from the cars that keep passing us, luggage racked on the roof sometimes, the dancing-with-death fast cars packed inside with seatfuls of blond-headed tourists, the license plates usually saying Deutschland on them, me having to bet my wife and losing almost every time a car passes, my wife saying, "What did I tell you, Germans, who else? Another pack of Germans trying to waltz into a ditch! Why aren't we swimming? We could have spent the whole day on the beach."

When what we bet were Germans are too far ahead for us to read their license plate anymore, we pass a woman dressed all in black, with a black kerchief tied around her head, walking on my side of the road behind a donkey, and hitting the donkey on the rump with a stick. "Going home," my wife says. "She's probably going home with a month's worth of groceries. Maybe it was donkey. Maybe they sliced us up some old donkey back there instead."

At the top of the mountain, where the road flattens out, we see water down below, in a valley with a few houses studded on the mountainside, topped with red roof tiles, and with a gravel road that winds up the mountain from somewhere down by what looks like a giant green lake stretched all the way out to the horizon between high mountains, looking to me, I say to my wife, like something dinosaurs came out of with their mouths full of algae. "Turn," my wife says. "Maybe someone down there will know. Maybe someone down in the village, down by the water. Go slow," my wife says, "it's all just gravel and rocks."

Going over whât is left of a rock slide on the road, I toss the white packet of wrapped meat out over the side of the mountain. "Maybe some bear will eat it and die," my wife says. "Some bear who knows where this stupid place is. Go slow," my wife says. "Please go slow!"

At the first house where I pull over and stop, there is no one coming out of the tile-roofed house or out of what looks like a barn when I call, and no one that I can see working in the small vineyard about the house, and in the village, the two little boys we talk to say they have never heard of a place called Jalce, and they laugh when my wife gives them each a dollar, and they try to give the paper bill back, and the woman at the grocery store says that she knows of some of our people in Titograd, to just go and ask any policeman on any corner in Titograd and to just tell the policeman the name, one of our people having been the former chief of police there, and to tell the retired chief, should I come to meet the gentleman, that Ange had sent us, Ange from Rijeka, Ange from the grocery store, Ange from Lake Skadar.

Before we get back into the car, I say that I want to go out onto that green water, where we can see a fishing boat now, moving slowly far away from the shore, and where an uncle drowned once, I say, and my wife says no, that she only likes it when the water is blue, and when there is sand and when there are no dinosaurs or dead uncles or rocks falling down all over our heads and then into that lizard water that looks to her like a dead sea, my wife says, full of fish fat with Germans trying to take the shortcut home to Deutschland, lizard water full of dead things at the bottom and fish that eat tires and air mattresses and chrome, just waiting for the next meal, the next thing to come falling off of the mountain. "Let's go! Let's go!" my wife says. "I do not want to be here when the sun goes down."

Graveling back up the mountain, I turn where there has been a rock slide, where I see the sign that we had passed before because the sign had said Ceklin and not Jalce, and now I turn because it is the last turn before the turn at the top onto asphalt, because the sun is still on our side, I say to my wife, and there is still time to look for this little handful of houses that they had always said was the place where my father was born, where my father said he had gone barefoot as a boy and even as a young man, this place somewhere in the mountains between Cetinje, where the king had lived, and Titograd, the city down on the plain, down on the other side of these mountains, where all of my people are waiting for us in the city house that the family has lived in for years now, I say, all waiting for us to just knock on the door and say the right name.

. . .

Looking up the side of the mountain, watching for the next loose spill of rock and dirt, we can hear the buzzing of things in the air and the wheels of the car turning over the stones underneath, the chalky-looking pieces of mountain slid down from the steep side of the cliff, and my wife tells me to go slow when we do not know where we are going, and that we are the only ones around here in a hurry, that we are the only ones around here at all.

After the big fender-scraping bump that sends the dust up, what we see ahead is a dark old board house set in from the road, with a woman dressed all in black sitting out by herself on the covered porch in front of an open space of window next to an open door, where we can see the trees and the dry grass in back through the back windows as we roll closer, a woman combing her long hair out slowly to one side, and when the car stops, there is only the sound of the car door opening and closing and the sound of my shoes on the gravelly dirt, and the buzzing. "Excuse me, madam," I say, in the language of my father that I have always spoken at home; "We are looking for Jalce, *selo* Jalce," I say, and the woman just keeps combing her hair and pulling out the strands to look at them, and then a dog comes to the doorway from the dark room inside. "Have you heard, madam, of this place that we are looking for, Jalce?" I say, in the form that I think is used for polite address, and then the woman takes up a thick strand and says after a down-combed, arm-length of a while, "Ceklin. This is Ceklin," the woman with the two or three front teeth

9

showing now says. "You have come to Ceklin." "We are looking for Jalce," I say. "*Selo* Jalce," I say, and then it is just the
buzzing in the air and in the dry grass and coming also maybe
from the shade tree by the house, the dry buzzing and the
woman holding up a little mirror from her lap and looking at
herself, the mirror in one hand and the comb still held in the
other hand, and the long hair streaked with the gray I can see,
folding down on one side of the woman's neck. "Ceklin," the
woman says, after looking at her smile in the mirror. "But
you have come to Ceklin."

Graveling back up the mountain, we stop when we see the
kind of Volkswagen that looks to me like a jeep, coming very
slowly down the mountain road in a low gear, the driver
wearing thin, metal-rimmed glasses and the blond woman
next to the driver, holding open a road atlas between them,
and I tell the driver, in English, that I can only say that he is
going the wrong way, if he wants to go to the ocean, and the
right way, if he wants to go to Lake Skadar, and the man says,
"Sorry, sorry," and then lets go of the brake. "Go slow," my
wife says, as we listen to the gravel grind underneath the tires,
and "Budva," my wife says, when we come to the sign that
points one way straight ahead into Titograd, and the other
way, on my wife's side of the car, toward Budva and the ocean,
and it is on this road, going down to the town just below Sveti
Stefan on the map, going down to Old Budva, closed off since

the earthquakes and cracked like a clay pot or looking to us
like a sand castle whose turrets have toppled and whose edges
have crumbled away, that we see, here and there, and then
again farther along, a car that has fallen into a wreck and sometimes gone belly-up down the side of the mountain, a car that
we make bets is either German or Italian, my wife not letting
me look back, even for a moment to make sure, but saying
every time that it was a German one back there, that it might
as well have been a German car, the way they drive, and telling me to keep my eyes on the road, us going down that long
wind of mountain back to the Magistrala, the coast road that
my wife says you do not need to be a gypsy with cards in order
to follow, the sun sinking an eye-burning disc of late summer
light into the glistening water out beyond the wide white beach
of Budva, a point of interest in the red guidebook with a para-
graph on the old walled city, the both of us saying all the things
we could think of to say later—that it was because we had ar-
ranged for the room after all, that the stonecutter had promised
to keep his best room ready for a young man going back to see
where his father had trod as a boy, we in a race to say all the
things that we could possibly tell them over the telephone, the
people waiting in the city on the plain on the other side of
the mountains for the son from America and his new wife,
waiting at some address every policeman was supposed to
know, we two saying now as the car waltzes around the
curves, that we could always say it was because we had already obliged ourselves to our host, to the man in suspenders

who had said that my people were somewhere up there for sure, ask any rock, the man had said, and that we just did not have a proper map, that was all, not any good map for this whole place, but just a walking map for Cetinje and the red guidebook showing a few points of interest and the sand or pebbled beach spots where all of the Germans and Italians planted their air mattresses, and that it had got to be night, and that we had made reservations for dinner at the beach, at that place that had been the summer villa of the king, and that we were just plain sorry to have missed them, that it would have to be another time, that we would have to make our acquaintance some other summer, and that we did not want to end up in a ditch or down with the dinosaurs at the bottom of the green cracked face of Skadar, down with that old family waiting for the next crunch of history to come graveling down off of the mountain, that family old as the Flood, my wife says, waiting for all of its lost sons to hurry back to the fatherland, still nibbling on those old green toes, on those floating feathery hands of the dead.

What My

Uncle Said

The uncle whom they always said I looked like, the youngest of the ones who came over in turns from the place that we always called Stari Krai, the old part of the world, the youngest of the three brothers and the sister and the sister's young husband, of all the ones who came over by way of France, the money for the ticket and the black market passport having been sent back by the first arrivals, until there had only been himself left of the ones who would leave the stone house again to work for foreign coin, my uncle said, the sister and the sister's young husband having been the first of the family to get to Paris since that time before the Balkan wars, when my grandfather had taken the oldest son of his nine children to dig a silver buck out of America in some Montana mine, the uncle who was the youngest of all the black-haired ones with eyes the same color blue as the crystal sea they had all crawled out of, that same uncle said, who had dug coal out of the low meadows of the Rocky Mountains of Canada, and who always made an arm muscle in front of my face and pulled my nose and said all the rest of it could go to hell, said that they had all walked down that black mountain back in Stari Krai by turns, walked down to Cetinje, nestled between the shoulders of the mountains and the first place that had roads good enough to keep a taxi in business, and had then paid the seventy-five dinars it took to roll the rest of the way down to the small town of Kotor, on the Bay of Kotor, taking the boat then, that ran along the coast from Kotor to Dubrovnik, and farther north to Split, and then to Trieste, where the Italians there could understand a Serb, boarding the train that ran from Trieste to Paris, in order to work to make enough money for the passage to America, the six-thousand-odd francs that it took then, and to meet those of our family and friends who had already learned how to say *du pain* and *l'argent*, to work in the factories that had a job for a foreigner—at Citroën, at Compagnie Durand, where they made window cranks for cars, and at the company where they sharpened saws—all living together, in time, at the same boardinghouse in the suburb of Levallois-Perret, where the French proprietor killed the dog one day to make the stew, the sister, my aunt, helping with the beds and the cleaning then, and with the cooking in the kitchen, telling the rest of ours not to eat all of what she had to ladle out, not to eat anything that was stuck hard to the bone, and then the bunch of them at last taking the big ships over, again in turns, as the quotas opened up, the hired agent placing the name of the eldest brother then in their number on the list for South America after the fifth year of work in France, and the sister and the young husband waiting the three years longer to get on the quota for the United States, where they would join up with friends from the husband's village, first in Pennsylvania, and later on in Butte, Montana, where there was a whole colony of our people working the coal and copper mines, and where my grandfather had first taken his eldest son and a cousin, stomach after bread, a good ten years before, leaving home to take up pick and shovel to dig for this green dollar, my grandfather going back to take care of the family again when work fell off, and the eldest son and the cousin putting down the pick and the shovel later, when the Turks had invaded the homeland and the country had called up all of her stray sons to fight, that eldest brother, my unseen uncle, destined to drown in later years in deep green waters, when the small boat taking a group of villagers to a funeral a mountain trek away turned its bottom up over the mourners, feeding the black-clad bodies like morsels to the fish-mouthed tangle of green strands below, the dressed-for-a-Sunday, black-clad ones who could not swim drowning in the green waters grassed with algae for fish-abounding miles between the high mountains, drowning in those grassed waters of the broad, veined lake of great Skadar, in that part of the black heights of Montenegro that looked like a valley of the moon, the two brothers then remaining in France, my father and himself, my youngest uncle, getting on the quota for Canada, paying the agent the through fare in advance to Edmonton, the hub for the mine fields as they had heard, out west where the Rockies grew up from the plain, they having gotten listed in the next year after the elder brother's ship had sailed for Argentina, from Cherbourg to Quebec City to Edmonton, province of Alberta, the two of them going second class on the sixteen-thousand-ton Alsonia, a ship of the Cunard line, to Canada, where the quota was as open as the one for heaven above, where the country was man-shy and glad to have any good back set to do work, and where the first work was a train ride across the continent away, laying down ties and track for the railroad at eighteen-cents-the-hour, my father being the first to get back on the train again and then onto the boat bound for Hyder, Alaska, to look for more work, my father saying later how he had gabbed at the ship's table like a baron until somebody had started to eat, he, my father, not knowing which of the forks to use first, or which of the spoons, the eldest brother coming up from South America to join his brothers, a year's worth of thin blue-papered airmail letters later, getting off the train at Sheraton, British Columbia, at one o'clock in the morning, his hands black for months afterward from having dug out roots for firewood in South America, and then he, my youngest uncle and the brother with the black hands, following in my father's tracks up to Alaska, where they all had work until the border-patrol man came around asking to look at visas, sending the brothers all three back out of that territory of the United States, back looking to land jobs in the coal mines of Alberta, spotted along the coal branch that the railroad had built out into the lower meadows of the Rockies, all three brothers soon digging together in the shafts of the Brule Mine for two years straight until the mine shut down, my father striking out alone again to look for gold mine work at Prince Rupert and then back east in Quebec, while the eldest brother and he, my youngest uncle, hunted down a month or two of shifts here and there among the timber-shack towns of the coal branch—at the town called Robb, at Mile Thirty-Two, and Mile Thirty-Three, and Mile Thirty-Four, at Mercoal, Shaw, Luscar and Coalspur, and finally at Cadomin, where there was enough work to settle down and put up a house, and where we would live as children later on, two brothers digging now next to Swedes and Russians and Germans and Poles at the bottom of those mountains tracked with deer and mountain antelope that you could knock down with a thirty-ought-six on a patch of days off, land run with bear and the wolverines who could put fear into a grizzly and who would eat the chickens running between the wooden houses and sun themselves on the slant doors of the cellars, until the eldest brother took himself that long way back to the black mountain in Stari Krai on money that he, my youngest uncle, had borrowed from a man at the mine from Bosnia, when Death had come pulling at the leg of that brother's son, gone from hurt to gangrene after a rock slide, leaving the two brothers remaining, my father and himself, my youngest uncle, to take the train down to California in the next year when Death had taken up the rope again, down to the California of what they had heard was all sun and sea and redwood, where the sister and her young husband had thought to place their new hopes then, down to marry off that suddenly newly widowed sister, according to tradition and to the trusts put upon male kin, to a man who was decent enough and who could provide, who could build that sister a home with his own skilled hands, after God had taken the hand of her first beloved, God and the wind blowing the mattress and the man off of the back of the moving van, to marry off that widowed sister to a man with a good trade, past his wilder years of playing cards on the side runners of his Buick coupe at Angel's Camp and up and down the mud banks of the Sacramento and the San Joaquin, when he could sport a brush of whiskers at some dance-doing in one of those small towns down the gut of California where our people had a piece of the land, a decent man, bald as a bumper, with the wild hairs of his youth paid out to scarlet fever, past those years when a brother on a visitor's visa would have to worry about a man tight with a pack of cards and loose after a skirt playing the wrong hand out, marry off that widowed sister to a man with a good automobile with the black and sun-yellow license plate of the great state of California clamped to the bumper, and having a few dollars to pocket, to marry off a sister and to have his elder brother, my father, dig up a wife along the way, my father sporting his suit and a pair of spats and a gold watch chain across a miner's thick chest on a Sunday outing to the farm where Old Chuze, my grandmother-to-be, ran a boardinghouse for the men who worked on the road gangs for the WPA, Old Chuze, whom my card-playing, road-laying future uncle knew from the old days of cutting roads up around the Stanislaus, who killed pigs and chickens and kept a victory garden and put out canned tomatoes and stew for the men cutting timber up the river or cutting roads out of the green gut of the state of California, Old Chuze, who had lost a good husband of her own to the river once, a timber walker who fell off one day when the logs had opened up and that river had taken a man-size swallow, and whose head never bobbed back up before the logs closed back tight again, Old Chuze, who had three beautiful daughters as he was told, that card-playing future uncle had said, he having seen but only a skirt here and there out around that old vineyard, the daughters always careful to keep closed doors and a vine row of distance away whenever the road men and the loggers were around the place, my father saying about the waitress who came over to the table in the roadside canteen that they had all stopped at on that hot, all-day ride out into the country—they being my father's sister, my aunt, and the new cement finisher in the family, the man who knew where all the roads in that long state connected, my father and himself, my youngest uncle—my father saying to the others when the waitress came over to the table, that he could make the sun and moon switch places given a half-night with this woman, and the woman, the waitress, asking back in that same other language that they had spoken between themselves, whether my father thought he might indeed be the better man for it in the morning, and my father running right out of the little roadside canteen then, to sit in the car, hanged as a dog, and wait for the others to pay the bill, and meeting that same woman standing on the oval rug at Old Chuze's place the half-shift later, the woman being the one of Old Chuze's daughters who read books and hid from the men in the vineyard, and who worked for skirt money with her older sister at that canteen down the road, my father coming back the Sunday next with a gold watch, a gold bracelet, a pair of small diamond earrings and a gold ring bought with Mother Earth's own money, saying that he was the manager of a big coal mine up in Canada and that he lived up there in the lap of God, in a green mountain meadow right under God's knees, capped with snow the year long—that good woman fetching up as just the ticket to marry up over a miner's handful of lost paydays under the California sun, and to pack up on a train and take back to the meadows of the Rockies to have his children, and to have the dinner ready, by God, and to have the water carried in from the well by the time my father came back from the mine, and to wash my father's black feet in the enamel basin, and to cook for my father and for whosoever of the other men would come to breakfast before the shift

in the mine started or to dinner when the shift was over, and
to hang out the clothes to dry on the line strung out to a tree,
until it was snakes that the woman was seeing in just your ordinary glass of water that a pair of scissors stood poked down in,
when the snakes had been only the cut curls of the bangs that
the woman had been trimming on the three little girls, my sisters, just bits of wet-down hair that had stuck to the scissors
dropped down into the glass of water, seeing the snakes and
then not wanting to eat and just lying down on the bed reading
the *Everyman's Encyclopedia*, until the widow sister and the
man who knew the roads, the man who put the finish on a piece
of concrete with rubber pads strapped over his kneecaps and a
set of trowels in his hands, and who laid sidewalk down in
front of new houses going up every day, until the widow sister
and that bald-as-a-bumper uncle came up to Canada in the
new black Buick, with strawberries and oranges and Pop-
sicles packed in the cooler, to take the three little girls in dresses
back down to the great state of California, the Golden State
of sun and blue ocean south to those tracks of jack pine and
snow winters, while my father took me and the woman seeing
snakes and reading the *Everyman's Encyclopedia*, down on the
train called the Northern Star, down through the mountains
and along the long coast to that city on the inland side of the
bay, darker at night than the big city across a gray span of
bridge that lay fingered between bay and ocean, down to the
city with a quiet lake in the middle and flat, spread-out neigh-

borhoods between the estuary and the hills, where my aunt lived in the big white house, the neighborhood that would be ours, being mostly still white, those fenced-in and flowered bungalows pretty well kept up by the people we would call the *furešti* just between ourselves, with some Portuguese, some Italians across the street and down, and a couple of Mexicans in the cheaper, one-story houses on the weed lots that were sick for paint, my aunt proud to own the big white two-story, just-about-prettiest house on the block, claw-hammered and rip-sawed up from the blueprints for one of those white stucco houses stuck in like teeth into the hard rock hills of San Francisco, blueprints only my card-playing uncle could make out, won in a game of poker it was only rumored, the big white house with the black-and-white hard granite stairs that looked like baby graves planted all in a row up some steep hill, and with the three slant-roofed and wall-married garages spread out at the back of the driveway, and roses growing all along the side of the house by the green slatted fence, and budding on the scissor-trimmed tall bushes growing in circles of cutout lawn in the front, the house with the deep backyard where my father planted a fig tree out by the T-pole of the clothesline, saying that he would not mind being the new gardener and keeping the garden out of weed, or doing whatever odd work was necessary around the place so that we could all have a nice home, now that my mother was gone, at a sisterly rate of rent, a roof over our heads that was at least of blood kin, and not the thin roof of one of those *furešti*, of some stranger, stranger to Mother Earth and stranger to woes, with a fair decent piece of ground outside the windows to raise up us kids, us Daddy-dawdled, rose-sniffing, empty-room-prowling pack of little lost wolves.

What My

Aunt Said

As she made the beds, tucking in the sheets with her fingers, I could hear the whispers that my aunt said the sheets made.

My aunt said, the sheets said, the whispers said:

Let your house catch on fire.

May your rock break into a hundred pieces.

May the rain drown your house.

May your legs break into a thousand pieces.

Let the fire catch you.

Let the snake drink at your eyes.

May your nose break.

Let the thunder break on your head.
Let the sun blind your wet eyes.
Let your gun explode.
My aunt said, the sheets said, the whispers said:
In the great white world.
In the world of the others.
My aunt said: *Stock, swine, Gypsy trash.*
My aunt said: *In the old corner of the world.*
My aunt said: *Of ours,* and, *one of ours.*
My aunt said: *Like your own house, like your own wife,*
                         and *like the mother who bore you.*
My aunt said: *Eyes on God, your eyes on God.*
My aunt said: *Sleep with the wolves, be like the wolves.*

The Walk

On days when my aunt would dig around the roses she grew along the side of the house, my aunt would say that the Devil was planting his agonies along with her, planting them in her back because he had run out of room in her heart. Then my aunt would pull herself up the stairs, holding on to the wooden handrail, and say that he would have to climb up into God's lap to get her, but in the meantime, that she had a cure. I would watch my aunt pick up the black telephone and slowly dial the number that she kept Scotch-taped in the cubbyhole in the wall where the telephone sat high on the shelf. "The Devil has the hoe," my aunt would say to the woman she would call when she had spent all day around the roses. "The Devil has the hoe again."

When the Devil had the hoe, my aunt would stand in front of the two tall pipes of the wall heater and turn up the dial, and wait for the woman who always wore black to bring the candles with her, the short candles like the ones in the colored glasses at church that took prayers up and burned your sins away, my aunt would tell me, the ones I always paid a quarter for and dropped into the blue cup. My aunt would put her candle into the little glass cup that was red, if she could find an empty one, because the burning wick in the red cup put God's light back into a heart, my aunt would say, as sure as any new rose, as sure as the Devil planted agonies in every hole God made.

When the woman who always wore black came up the back stairs with the candles and the oil wrapped up in a sack, I would stand by the dining-room table and watch my aunt unbutton the front buttons of her housedress, and raise each shoulder up first to pull her arms out of the armholes, one arm and then the other, and I would listen to my aunt make a moan sound as she pulled each side of the dress down toward the thin belt around her waist. Then my aunt would lie down on her stomach in front of the wall heater, with her cheek against the carpet, which had the shapes of leaves in it, dark and light, in shades that my aunt told the ladies who came to visit, were colors of rose. I would listen to my aunt moan as the woman who always wore black stood up barefoot on top of my aunt's back and walked over all the places where my aunt said that it felt like a hoe digging in. To me, it looked as if the two tall pipes were the trunk of a tree that my aunt had fallen from, and that my aunt was lying down on the bed of leaves where she had fallen, listening with one ear down, to the sounds in her that she said God and the Devil both made.

While my aunt lay on the rose-colored leaves that stood out from the carpet, the woman in black would walk every-where she could put her feet down on top of my aunt's back and not fall off from, and I walked alongside her, so that the woman in black could put her hand on top of my head and go easy and one-hand lighter, the woman in black said, go easy where she had to put her feet down and one-hand lighter where the Devil hoed.

"Where is it?" the woman in black would say, as if she might be stepping on the hoe just that second.

"There, there," my aunt said, as I made the same close-together steps on the carpet that I could see the woman in black making, when I looked with only my eyes looking down.

"Easy-slow, easy-slow," the woman in black said, and I could see her heels digging in first and then the toes reaching out to pull the skin in and hold on to it, and I could feel my toes doing the same inside my shoes, walking on the carpet, as if I could pull the leaves in if I wanted to. "Easy-slow, easy-slow," the woman in black said, as I watched her feet

28

move close together all along and down into the little row that curved down toward where the dress was pulled back over the thin belt. Then came the few steps extra, always at the bottom, a few more steps to put the Devil out of business, the woman would say, when the woman would put the other hand on top of my head, the way that the priest at church would do it, and say the "Easy-slow" for both of us to turn around.

When the woman in black had walked on all the places where my aunt had said she could feel the hoe, I watched the woman unhook my aunt's brassiere and pull the straps away to the sides, and I could see the white skin curve down into a row along my aunt's back to where her dress rolled back over the belt.

"He's looking for my soul," I heard my aunt say. "He's still digging around someplace for it."

Me, I would have to look for glasses in the kitchen then, the thickest ones we had, the woman in black would tell me. Glasses to pull the agonies out.

I would give the woman the thickest ones, the monkey glasses that I used to pour my milk into and that my aunt used for juice. I gave the woman in black all six of the short, thick glasses that had yellow monkeys on them, going around the top, and brown monkeys going around the bottom. The yellow monkeys hung down their tails from the branch and the brown monkeys did the same, hanging upside-down underneath the yellow monkeys, so that their tails hooked, dark around light and light around dark, in the middle of the glass, and so that any way the glass stood, full or empty, half the monkeys always looked as if they might fall on their heads if the monkeys on top let go.

I would watch the woman in black light the short candles and put six of them down on top of my aunt's back, on both sides of where the white skin went down in a row, and then put the monkey glasses on top of each candle so that this time it was the yellow monkeys who looked as if they might fall, and the brown monkeys who looked as if they had already had their turn.

"Now it will be better," the woman in black said, as I listened to the hollow sounds that the two tall pipes of the heater made and as I watched the tops of the glasses cloud with smoke as the candles burned and went out.

"Now we will see," the woman said, as I watched the yellow monkeys hang upside-down under the little trees of smoke that the burnt wicks made, and as the bumps of skin started coming up into each glass, where my aunt would say the Devil was digging his row then, the way the Devil had already dug and planted his agonies in her heart.

I would watch my aunt's white skin, the smooth mounds of it that moved up slowly inside the glasses where the candles had burned and then gone out, the way I had seen the candles go out at church when they had burned a quarter's worth of sins away in the colored cups, and I would sit down on the ottoman and wait for the monkeys to let go, for the woman in black to wiggle the glasses back and forth and let the air in. And I would wait for the skin to fall back the way it always was on my aunt's body, when it was just me and my aunt and not the woman in black with her candles and the oil she rubbed in afterward, and nothing there shaped different that anyone could call the Devil, pushing up with his hell-burnt head to blow out God's light.

Waiting for the UPS

The time my sisters went away to live with near relations, I stayed behind where my aunt said it would be better for us both now, in the backyard that would be better for me now to play in, would have more room for me now to go around in, without my sisters doll-dickering around in it, taking up all her sheet-room on the clothesline and messing up the downstairs, where my sisters slept, with their doll-dickering, Gypsy-trinket little things to trink up her mind with, all their wild-filled petticoats, flapping up out there over the fence, yapping back to her any which way the wind blew.

I stayed behind and played in all the room we had outside, under the peach tree and the apricot tree that had bricks
going all around them at the bottom, and under the fig tree just
inside the back fence, the real tree growing next to the tall
wooden T-pole that my aunt had up for the clothesline, the
thing that looked to me as if it had been a tree once, with more
on it than just the one wooden arm now, going across straight
just under the top, like a telephone pole wired up for the
wash.

I played in the long T-shadowed backyard, on the
smooth cement patio that went all the way back to the brick-
bordered garden my aunt had for onions or tomatoes or beans,
growing up sticks under the clothesline that wired the sky
between the tall wooden T-pole in the back of the garden
and the shorter, double-folded-sheet-length-to-the-ground-high
version of it, stuck down in cement behind the house, where my
aunt would stand with the basket on the ground, full of wet
wash, pinching together the cold corners of the sheets under
the wooden clothespins and inching the rabbit-eared wooden
pins out, hand over hand, on the wire that looped over pulley
wheels at the ends of the crossbar, sending the sheets out to
blow high over the green garden, and lower over the green-
slatted fence that married the long side of the backyard to the
one next door.

I rode my bike-car in all the billowy room under the
sheets, flapping over the smooth cement that went all over
to the brick borders, the patio grooved into squares where grass

33

had grown before my uncle poured and troweled smooth the cement right up to the back of the house, rode in all the washed-out air there was around and under the sheets when the wind was blowing the sheets up over the green-slatted fence, before they swooshed or snapped back down again onto our side, down onto my head, me going in the bike-car between and under the flaps as far and as fast as I could go before I would hit the brick-walled end of all that room that was not enough room to hang another petticoat in, my aunt would say, and the sky-filled white sheets would double-back down in a swoop and wrap a wind-folded sleeve around my head, as if we were playing blindman's buff.

I would ride my bike-car under the sheets and around all the places that my uncle could bend a brick around, that my uncle could put a powdery, chipped red wall up to, three bricks high all along the fence where the sheets blew over the roses that the caterpillars climbed up green sticks to eat, the caterpillars that ended up over the green fence in Jenny Dove's mouth when there wasn't another petticoat around on either side of the fence to stop Jenny Dove and the sheets were driving the driver around mad, making the blindman go where the sheets wanted him to go, the blindman thought, blind into their white, wind-wrapped arms.

Going under and in between, whenever it was my turn to have to look, I could sometimes see Jenny Dove put her

girl arms through the green-slatted fence and pull the caterpillars off the roses between flaps, and bite one in two with
her front teeth, no matter which way the wind was blowing,
and I would sometimes see Jenny Dove throw the other half
back—the part that still moved as if it had a mind of its own—
back into the dirt under the roses or onto the smooth cement,
where I would make my bike-car go around the furry, yellow-
green stub end if I could, riding under my aunt's white, wet-
wash-wedded sheets, flapping over at the corners like a woman flaps over a skirt to show off her legs, showing me Jenny
Dove behind the green-slatted fence, pulling the roses toward
her through the green slats with her naked girl arms.

When my aunt would come out to touch, to take up a sheet by
the corner to see what the air was doing, my aunt would see
the half-things on the smooth cement, or hanging off the edge
of a brick, and I would listen to my aunt call Jenny Dove's
mother to the back kitchen window that looked out over our
backyard, and tell Jenny Dove's mother that this dickering
would have to stop, that this dickering with the roses would
have to cease, that there were limits, not to mention the child's
health, limits to letting things run all to the Gypsies every
which way in front of your eyes when there was a window to
keep a look on things, and plenty of good soap and water
around to wash the wildness out.

　　Then I would watch Jenny Dove go inside the back-porch door, with a "half a mind to whip you, Jenny Dove," go inside to have to wait, the way I would wait all day for my father, wait for her father to come home in the UPS truck, the man we called just Hank instead of Mr. Dove and the man who called Jenny Dove "Little Sister," the man who Jenny Dove's mother would tell my aunt, out of the back kitchen window, was just the right person to put a mind on the matter, and not anyone else, and that there wasn't anything in the world that couldn't wait until five o'clock, that the world wasn't running all that wild yet, anyway, and that there was nothing out there that she could not come right on over and sweep up in a minute.

I rode around in the T-shadowed backyard, over the wet marks where a broom and a half-bitten thing had been, where the sheets were billowing dry. I rode around the peach tree and the apricot tree, where you could still see a caterpillar or two, branch-high on the bark, the same caterpillars that would cross over the patio at night to leaf over to a rose, the way the shadow of the T-pole moved across the green garden and out past the shadows of the sheets, like the spine of a giant leaf, bitten down to a T-shape, bitten all the way down to perfection.

I rode around in all the green-slatted room we had out back and around the house, around to the front where I could see if my father was coming, or if the UPS truck was coming, or if it was just the slow-as-a-square-wheel junkman, sputtering past every house that had a fence, saying, "Hey, Pete . . . Heya, Pete!" out of the junk-truck window, slow enough for the ladies to run out with a dead toaster or an old iron. I rode around in the bike-car until there wasn't any more riding to do, until it was maybe just trying to stay on the slats running between the tomatoes and the beans, or until it was just all right to just sit on a brick for a while, down by the roses, and wait for Hank Dove to turn the big, brown UPS truck into the driveway next door and roll it all the way in up to the chipped white wooden doors of the garage and stop.

When the big brown UPS truck would roll all the way back in past all the roses along the house, my aunt would come out of the back-porch door with her basket and put it down in front of the short T-pole, where the wire came down close enough to reach, and I would watch my aunt pull them back in, all the dry, blown-through ones, flapped-out quiet, like nuns coming home from church, coming away from the big cross to the little cross they kept on the wall at home, quiet with their sins washed clean.

And I would watch Hank Dove just sit there for a while, with his naked-muscle arm, elbow up on the big steering wheel behind the slide-door window of the brown UPS truck, as if he was thinking, just only thinking and sitting all quiet in the driver's seat, waiting for the last nun to go in. And I could see the part of Jenny Dove's mother, moving in the back

37

kitchen window, quiet behind glass, the part covered by a frilly apron with dots on it—just that part of her moving, and sometimes her head bending down.

Then I would watch Hank Dove slide open the cabin door of the UPS truck, when there were only shadows of wires and poles to look at on our side of the fence, and I would say, "Hi, Hank," and he would cross up quick to the back-porch door wearing his dark brown UPS uniform, and go in until I could see just that part of him from the waist up and from the head down, and I would see Hank Dove fall forward into the frame of the window with an arm stretched out in front of him, like one of those soldiers you would see in the movies, coming back home and hanging off a train—soldiers home for good, falling and falling forward into the crowd, falling toward their mothers and their sisters and their wives, like blind men, falling into arms they know.

Eternity

Whenever the ladies came over for orange sponge cake and sugar doughnuts and my aunt's pot-boiled coffee, my aunt would tell the ladies about the Hard Time and pull the picture album out of the bottom drawer of the dining-room dresser to show the ladies the black-and-white truth of it, of how she had lived through the Hard Time when God decided to change around all the furniture on her and stick her in her own garage to live like a rabbit without a man's hand to help and to throw out the white trash who would not pay the rent, living spread out in her own house in the front—whenever my aunt would tell

the going-to-the-store-dressed-up ladies the black-and-white
truth of what God had done to her during the Hard Time,
I would dunk my doughnut moon into my cream-muddied
coffee cup or soak my yellow wedge of sponge cake until it
fell back down into the ocean out of the plane, when I tried
to put the piece back into my mouth, and I would go back
with my spoon to get the man out of the water or the fallen
piece of moon out of the lake, while my aunt told the ladies
how God had choked her whole soul red on her chest, red as
a robin's, when God had reached down like a blind eagle and
pulled her young husband off the back of the furniture truck,
together with an old mattress and a couple of loose-tied chairs
piled up in a heap, just as the truck was turning the corner
sharp, and had married that young head to the high curb for
all eternity, and had come back then with those same hard
talons, all during the Hard Time, to claw, every odd-found
moment of the day or of the night since that funeral, black
and white told as truth still is, to claw on the place where
God must have thought there was a stick or two of something
still left, right there—my aunt would point down to the V of
her dress—where my aunt said she had to take her God-
loosened, heart-dropped breath.

While my aunt passed the book around the table so that all
the ladies could see the pictures stuck into little black V's at
each corner, all the pictures passed lady to lady around the

table and passed right past me, dunking my last drink of moon or getting my drowned man out of the water before he melted into just mud at the bottom of the ocean, I could hear my aunt tell the ladies what a person would have to be inside her bones to know the hollow-hard truth about the red her chest was under that long black veil, there, standing in the middle behind the casket, with all the men who were on that rickety tied-together truck, and there, standing alone like somebody's black angel behind her dear departed, with a hand on the spray bed of flowers and a hand on the open lid as though she had just opened a package, and there, the dark one of her standing behind the new-bought thick curve of smooth polished stone, the black veil draped over her face and over her chest and just brushing the top of the black, curved-down stone that always looked to her like the turned-down hollow mouth on a mask of tragedy, the pictures that my aunt said were only the beginning of the Hard Time, that nobody knew better to tell of than she did, not any one of those lank-necktied, dark-suited men in the back, nor any of those to her close, all grouped around the casket and around the three-legged, propped-up standing circle wreaths, the people who only knew the outside part, like the dumb difference between head and rock or fast or slow around a corner, and none of the truth that only she and this one God knew, as black and as white as any picture she could point to between those loose black pages, the Hard-Time-lived-through truth that only a woman bereaved by a young-fallen-down husband gets to know in a cold rabbit room in back, with whatever clawed God we had for a father coming back to her red-rashed chest the whole long length of those years buried, like some eagle great for the small thing it had dropped.

While the ladies passed the black picture album around the table and then back to my aunt to turn the page, I could see one or two of the ladies make a few tears and reach up with a folded paper napkin or into the snap purse, hung from the back of a dining-room chair, for a flower-stitched handkerchief, and dab an eye or wipe a little at the bottom of a nose and make a sniff sound, and after I had dunked the muddy lake dry or drowned the last bit of man in the ocean, I would go into the kitchen to see if there were any more doughnuts left in the bag for later, before I got my marble men out of the bottom drawer in the bedroom and put them in the glass ashtrays that I used for boats on the all-over rose carpet, and slid the glass-bottomed boats in all the water around the table that had the nyloned, open-toe-clunk-heel-shoed feet of the ladies in it, and the legs of the table and the legs of the chairs that I said were lighthouses or trees on an island or just big rocks or icebergs to stay away from on a long glide across the water, where always a marble man or two would fall out of a packed-loose-on-purpose boat, so that I could come by and do the rescue with my one marble man, alone in his boat, the glass boat I had to keep my hand on the whole way out to the drowning men, because the one man would never stay put in a fast-stopped boat, gliding on the ocean, but would jump out at the end of the ride, and drown with the men he was only sent out to save.

Sometimes, when my aunt was pouring out the second or third cup that the ladies always stayed over to have so that they could hear about the Hard Time and how it all was or so that they could give what one or two of the ladies would always call their block-walked-off nyloned legs a rest, I would crash my ashtray boat of marble men into a lighthouse leg of table so that most of the men would jump out and have to swim until I crawled under the table to do my rescue, and some one or two of the ladies who always came over for orange sponge cake and doughnuts would reach into a snap-shut purse and drop a dime or a nickel or even a quarter for me to rescue up and keep for being such a little lifesaver, such a little lifesaver for a hardworking woman with a young husband long laid down under a rock.

And sometimes the big woman in black who always sat at the end of the table and smelled of perfume and wore the orangy-brown, fox-looking things that bit themselves in a circle around her neck, sometimes the big woman would put her big foot down on a marble man swimming and tell me that she knew just what kind of a no-good captain I was, who would look up a lady's dress quick as any sailor if he did not get a drop of something in his ocean, and then the big woman would reach into her chair-hung black purse and pull out the little paper packet with the purple flaky rocks inside, and bite off a white V-corner and pull the bit of paper from between her teeth, and pour out a little purple pile of flaky rocks into each of my palms for me to lick them wet, and then pour out a little for herself to wet-touch to her tongue, putting the packet then back into her purse, the purple flaky rocks that tasted to me like grapes that I licked down to just a purple blotch on each hand, and that I then said was my blood and where I was wounded, me rolling off of the couch onto the rose carpet, or off of my bed in the bedroom while the ladies made little tongue and teeth sounds as the picture book went around the table, little cluck sounds as I fell out of planes and off the backs of trucks onto the all-over rose carpet so that I could be down for a while with the men drowning and not always the man left behind, doing all the saving, or when I was being just a young dead husband, picked up and dropped by some eagle over the ocean, down dead on the rock furniture at the mud bottom where the world is only water, waiting for my young wife to die and to swim down to my rock table and to my rock chairs and to my rock bed, waiting in eternity for the ladies to finish drinking the muddied-up coffee and to stop making little cluck sounds looking at the black-and-white truth, waiting the long hard time for my aunt to clear the table and to finish doing the dishes in the sink, when my aunt would come over and pretend to find me and then pull me up with a tug, me wounded and me drowning and me dead at the mud bottom of the world, and then me up quicker than ever I wanted when my aunt would stand over me in her open-toed shoes and reach down and pull me back to her off of the all-over rose carpet that was the water of the world, me out of my aunt's boy-tall hat like any quick-snatched rabbit saved for the end of the show, saved up for the last surprise.

To France

I played teatime and paper doll dress-up with my youngest sister on the sand-colored, nap-naked-to-thread-in-places front-room rug with the black hooked lines in it spaced around the border that curved in toward the big black diamond island in the middle like coat hooks or anchors that you could call your harbors, or the places where your doll-boy lived or your doll-man kept his car parked or his ship docked, or that you could call just your places to hook the teacup when the tea party that day was on your side of the world.

Whenever my aunt came in with the stand-up vacuum
or with the string mop to do the linoleum tiles that went the
whole way to the wall, my youngest sister and I went to other
parts of the world with the doll-people, on sudden trips we
said they had to take, on holidays by train or by airplane or
boat to the places away from my aunt that my aunt said we
could play in if there was not the clutter to have to look at,
the loose and useless scattered over every corner to have to
come sweep up and hands-and-knees scrub over without the
help of spoiled hands idle to do the real work about the house,
the corner-to-corner necessary to keep this family out of dirt
and people's mouths so that people could only say clean about
how we lived and not say how we lived like motherless wolf-
children without a bed to sleep in or anyone there to look
after the comings and goings, the places we could go to in the
house a room ahead of my aunt with the duster or with the
stand-up vacuum or with just a rag of torn-up dress, or the
longer, across-the-whole-Atlantic-and-Pacific trips we made
the doll-people take to our place in the corner of the last-
over garage from the garden, the last-over one of the three
wall-married garages in the backyard that had the wine barrels racked up in rows behind the big wooden doors, the place
my aunt said it was all right for us to play in so long as my
sisters kept their hollow-headed, blinking rag babies out of
the way of my uncle coming in to fill up the wine gallon for
supper or to pull a head of sour cabbage out of the brine bar-

rel, or so long as my sisters kept out of the way of her broom, whenever it was my aunt's high-time-as-any to sweep the cobwebs down out of the rafters, all right to play in if we kept foolish-and-hollow strict to a corner and not spread funny-papered and stuck all over creation, not even hers but my uncle's, for him to have to come home to after work and have to look at, staring back at him out of the next to dark—the funny book tepeed over a gunnysack-wrapped wood stopper, or the hollow-headed, stranger-orphaned rag baby, left cradled-down in nobody's good bed for clutter, between the ring-wrapped ribs of my uncle's hammer-and chisel-knocked-tight full barrels.

Those days when we had the things that somebody could call just clutter, the used funny books and the blinky-eyed dolls that my sisters got hand-me-down from the half-Indian brother and sister around the corner, and the pink tin tea set and paper doll-people that we got from the fat girl who got everything up the street, what I had hollow was a red and blue drum that an auntie lady in San Francisco had reached down out of the closet for me to take home to practice on, the drum my aunt said it made her nervous all up the arms just to look at, that gave her a headache to have to think about it being in the house at all, so that it belonged only in the place in the garage and not anywhere in the house or the backyard, so that she would have to hear it or think about it and get nervous in her arms when she had to do the work—those days we would listen for the sound of the keys jangling before my aunt ever turned a corner or opened a door.

We would listen for the house keys and the garage keys that my aunt kept on a safety pin pinned to her housedress or to the blue button-up wool sweater that my aunt wore even mornings in the summer, that we called the policeman sweater, because it had all the keys on it to the locked places away from the house and away from my aunt, where my aunt said it was all right to play in if there was not any work for my sisters to do, the keys we could hear jangling whenever my aunt would come down the stairs or walk up the driveway with the groceries or come outside of the porch to dig around the garden or to unlock the washroom, the silver and gold bunch pinned just above a hip sweater pocket, like a loose-dangling badge.

Those days when I had the red and blue drum, so that it was not just tea party or paper doll dress-up to play, or putting the doll-babies to sleep between the barrels, I played on the drum and on the ends of the barrels with the sticks, behind the pulled-shut, drop-bolt-dragging wooden garage doors with the gauzy curtains over the high little square windows, while my sisters looked at the funny books by the little-lined light through the curtains on the doors and by the light of the glowing hair wires of the clear glass bulb, dangling down from the rafters over the barrels, and the paper doll-people just stayed in the box, in France, where we always said they had to go when it was not doll dress-up time anymore.

The day that nobody listened good enough, when the doll-people were in the box, in France, and my youngest sister had sat the doll-babies up to tea and my other sisters were stacking up the funny books to trade, when I was riding up on top of the hollowest-sounding barrel with the wood spigot hammered in at the bottom, my aunt pulled back the drop-bolt-dragging big wooden door with nobody hearing, with nobody listening any good enough for the keys, and said that her keg was knock-full-to-bust with all the noise of drums and clutter and that there was no room in her house for blinky-eyed, nothing-home-in-the-head babies, orphaned over a fence, and that she was not going to stay in the house all day nervous in the arms with all the work anymore, while we fooled all day in the dark with other people's giveaway, like wolf-children holed up in a den.

I watched my aunt wave the broom at my sisters then, and tell them to stand back away from her work, away from the corner-to-corner that she was going to sweep so that nobody could say anything about the dust on her carpet or about anybody else's giveaway stacked up under her roof. I watched from my place on top of the wood-cork-stoppered wine barrel while my aunt swept the pink tin tea set out into the ocean, out into what we said was the whole Atlantic and Pacific, and swept the broom over the top of the stack of funny books in the corner and at the doll-babies sat-up on the smooth cement floor, until all the arms and legs and heads and buttoned-on dresses were broom-rolled under and around the tumbled tepee huts of funny-book covers and broken-off baby brooms of straw, out into the square-grooved cement yard outside of the bolt-dragging door, where we said it was all ocean, swiping now and again at my sisters' shoes with the red-string-plaited straw-head of the broom and hitting the broom handle against a moving shin whenever one of my sisters tried to grab her doll-baby back, until my sisters were all three backed up against the drumheads of the bigger-galloned barrels in back, that my uncle said had sap enough still to put some good years on his wine, and I put the knob-tipped sticks to the drum down the leg of my pants how I could, before my aunt said that I had to get down off of the barrel, down into the corners that I had dirtied up with my sisters to carry my good weight of trash over to the curved-top brick barbecue pit where it belonged, where she had a proper place for it, while my aunt picked up the doll-babies by the legs, one in each hand until all of the doll-babies had had their turn, and knocked the blinky-eyed heads against the trunks of the fruit trees, the way that my aunt knocked the wet string mop against the trunk of a tree to make the gray strings fall down right, saying that she had no room left for other people's loose-and-useless tossed over her fence and for any more hollow heads to feed, dragged out of every dark corner, and that she was going to get out all the cobwebs this time for good, all the nerves back down to quiet in her arms.

I watched my aunt poke the broom handle then, through both stretched sides of the red and blue drum until the part in the middle flapped around the rim like paper, and then I watched my aunt take the hollow tin rim part and throw it into the brick barbecue pit where the top curved around like a barrel, and then throw into the black-bricked hole the yard-scattered, rolled-to-a-stop handful of head or the still-dangling-by-a-neck-string, trunk-tomahawked cracked head and gauzy dressed-up rest of the dolls.

Going back inside the wine-barrel garage to get what armful I could carry of the hand-me-down funny books stacked in the corner, I saw my youngest sister take the doll-people in the box, in France, and put them in what we said were other parts of the world, not any good for holidays by train or boat or plane across any land or water in the world, but places where we said the spiders lived and made their webs behind the bigger-galloned old oak barrels where my aunt could never reach right with the broom.

Carrying what I could carry and still walk with the sticks stuck down, I watched while my aunt stood at the black-bricked hole of the barbecue pit, lighting the corners of the funny books with the wood matches that she carried in her sweater pocket to light the stove with, until my aunt said that nobody would eat until she got the sticks to the drum that I reached down then and held out to her, and that my aunt tapped lightly together then against one of the fruit trees, saying that that would be the last time anyone would send her their drum to march by and make her all nervous in the arms, and set me up the drummer to tap her down a day too early into this green garden.

We watched what we had that somebody could call clutter burn up then in the curved-top brick barbecue pit, while my aunt locked up the last-over garage with one of the jangling keys on the safety pin and walked back into the porch room with a last door-stoop whack of the broom.

My uncle said it was all just trash and paper gone and that a drum was just a barrel with nothing good in it, and that he had twenty drums lined up that I could play on if I wanted to with his fat yellow carpenter pencils or with his flat paint sticks, if I liked that sound any better, that I could tap on the barrels with when it was just the two of us before dinner, behind the pulled-in shut, bolt-dragging doors, me holding up the gallon jug under the wooden, knocked-in spigot until the wine had trickled up the neck to full, and my uncle, lifting off the heavy, white-marbled, smooth rounded stone, set on top of the wood blocks stacked up on the sunk-down, waterlogged lid of the sour-cabbage barrel, reaching down with the naked, rolled-up-sleeve hook of his arm into the salt-foam-floating water for the big soft one sleeping at the bottom, my uncle said, sleeping under the head-soaked weight of his brothers and his sisters, like a spoiled-fat baby swelling up sweet on brine, rolled up in snug harbor waiting for the tide to change, waiting for his trip to France.

All the Green

Turns Back

Where my mother was, they said, was a place behind trees that you could get to if you just went straight, if you did not turn in front of the tall gray factory set back off the road that had a dark field of cows and the smell of cows around it. If you just went straight a little farther, instead of turning where we always turned, where the road went past the tin-gray factory, past the cows that grazed in front and the tin-and-wet-dung smell that the factory made, you would get, instead, to a clump of trees that had my mother someplace behind it, in a building that you could see a little above the treetops like a tower of cream.

We never did go straight but only turned, past the cows that stood out there where the smell was, so that it was how much breath you had, how long you could hold the good air in without letting any of it out, without having to let even a little of the tin-and-dung air in—how many fence posts it took to fret the wires, front windshield to back, the sometimes leaned-way-over-sideways sticks you could hear your heart count as they passed by, before you let go, just a few sticks at a time, let go of the long boy-ribbed breath you were holding inside as the cows passed by in rolled-up window pictures of cows standing in groups behind the thin, loose strands of poke-wire fence that my uncle told me was all that was required to keep a dumb cow in.

This is where we turned, where the tall trees started in a row if you just kept going straight ahead, one after another evenly apart all along my mother's side of the road, they told me, until the tall trees would start to clump together farther on. This is where we turned away to go to the farm, me in the front seat and my sisters in the back with my father, who always brought a hat whenever he was going for a visit, and rolled the brim around in his lap—me in front, between my uncle and my aunt, holding my breath until we had passed the worst part of the tin-and-dung smell around our mother, and the kid who did not laugh and let any breath go, the kid who could keep the dung air out of his lungs, won the ice cream at the last stop.

The next stop was where my uncle said it could be, and sometimes it was at the Fat Boy, and sometimes it was just at a turn in the road where you could stop to pee. When it was at the Fat Boy, my uncle and my father would walk me across the street to pee in the Toilet For Men in the saloon where the Mexicans were. My aunt said it was no place for a woman to go, no place for a woman to sit anywhere down in, so my aunt and my sisters just stayed in the car and waited for me and my father and my uncle and for the next blind turn in the road where the grass looked right.

Whenever I wanted to go inside where the Mexicans were, where it was dark always at first and where I could push my shoes through the sawdust on the floor, I told my uncle that I could not hold it in anymore and that the grass did not look somehow right and my uncle would say to my aunt that the Fat Boy was as good a place as any to stop and give the motor a rest and to do something to kill the smell.

While my uncle and my father stood at the bar with the Mexicans—doing a little something, my uncle would tell the bartender, to kill the smell—I pushed my way back to the Toilet For Men, past the long smooth-topped tables where the Mexicans were pushing around the shiny black things that looked to me like ashtrays. I pushed with my toes through the sawdust on the floor all the way back to the Toilet For Men, so that I could see the sign up on the back wall up close, the sign with the hollowed half moon in it lit up yellow and the stars in it, flickering white, and the girl sitting down in the hollowed half-curve of the moon, with one leg crossed over the other leg, as if she were sitting down in a swing, taking a slow ride, it looked to me, a long slow ride through the stars—the girl that my father would always call my girlfriend whenever I went back to pee and to look up close and that my father would always tell me was not anywhere at all as good-looking as the young woman he had scooped up for life.

I would look up at the sign, at what the Mexicans had for a moon, and at the girl that my father said was not any-where at all as good-looking as the one that was still my mother, the one that my father said he had married when she was still a young woman, and that my father went back alone to see whenever we would drive out weekends to the farm.

Then I would take the long breath it would take to go in and pee, looking down until the pee would almost stop, and then I would give up looking for a place where the good air was and just let the air that was in there in—the lemon-yellow-smelling smell of the Toilet For Men and the smell that the Mexicans brought in with them, I thought, caked on in heeled-up cow dirt stuck behind the leaned-way-under heels of the cowboy boots that the Mexicans clumped up the saw-dust with, dirt you could see when one of the Mexicans came into the Toilet For Men and stood a boot next to you and made a sound with his breath and in his throat, and pushed the little, lemon-yellow smell thing around the poke-holed bottom of where the pee trickled down into with the wet tip of the other boot.

I would walk back then, straight past the long, smooth-topped table where the Mexicans were still pushing the shiny black things past each other, to the place where my father stood next to my uncle at the bar—my father, holding his hat in his hand—and I would see my uncle push a fifty-cent piece past the little empty shot glass that he had on the bar in front of him, and past the little glass in front of my father that looked almost full, and I would sometimes hear my uncle say to my father not to keep standing there, looking at something or nothing, but to just kill it, so that we could all get going again.

Outside, there would always be someone who could not wait for the grass to get any greener, and then we would all have to sit in the car in the parking lot behind the Fat Boy and wait for one of my sisters or for my aunt to finish what she was squatting down and doing, the thing it was better to do in an open field of tall cow grass than to sit down and do with a Mexican, my aunt would tell my uncle whenever it would be my aunt's turn to come out of the grass, keeping us all waiting, or even when it would be my uncle's turn instead, holding up the works on her, backing into the car butt first behind the wheel, with his shift hand holding his hat on and the other hand pulling the door in shut, saying that he had killed maybe but only one or two in there, just to chase the smell out of his head.

Then my uncle would turn the white knob around until the side window was down on his side and then he would turn the white steering wheel around the way my uncle said it was only his business to turn it, and we would get back onto the road going to the farm with what my uncle told us was the God-green smell of what they grew around here to feed the cows with streaming through the windows, my uncle saying that the tin-and-dung smell of the factory was too many turns and too many fence posts back then to make a tin cow's bit of difference anymore. And I would turn around in the front seat and look over at my father, sitting with his hat in his lap, next to the window, and my father would say something like pretty soon, or pretty soon now, sonny, that we would pretty soon get to the store in town where they sold nails in barrels and where my father would get out to wait for the yellow bus to take him all the green turns back to the place behind trees, when my father would have to bend over to get out of the backseat and hold his hat out in front of him, so that he would not crush it, doing things the way my father said he wanted to do things until things got a little bit different—get out and give my biggest sister the money to make every kid a double-dip winner, and put his hat on his head, and thumb along the brim in front, and stand there, waiting for us to get them at the drive-in dairy across the street, the soft-swirled little towers of ice cream that we waved out of the rolled-down windows of the car—me then, crawled over into the place where my father had been in the backseat with my sisters, me waving the thing melting out in the car wind going away, and my father just sitting down on a barrel or a bench, looking like any other man, waiting for the next long slow-turning thing to come.

What They Said

the Leaves Were

The first day on the farm, I built a house out of the things of the garden, the long, dry fronds they told me came from plants that were sun-dead now, a dead thresh of sun-spoiled leaf just only good for mulch, with a few thumb-thimblefuls of blood-red strawberries still alive in the shade of overlapped fronds, touching and all spread out over the dried-out dirt, like the hat-faced Mexicans I had seen from the car, dozing under a peach-bald or a plum-bald, picked-to-the-nub fruit tree, that had had the hands of a whole family on it, and then the hands and arms and legs of a whole family resting under it, one touching somewhere the other, it looked to me, like hair, like roots spread out—the women looking out at the cars passing on the road, with their skirts spread out over a furrow, and a small head sleeping here and there where the trees of the women came together, like fruit that had fallen down on its own that the women had gathered up into their skirts—the bruised fruit that my uncle told me was all right for a family of these people to take home, wrapped into a shirt or pulled up into a skirt—the plow-fruit pulled down by the hand of God alone and not by the black-nailed, knuckle-stiff thumb of some Mexican.

I built a house, a place to go into just far enough away to see the white-board house spread out from side to side between trees and bushes whole, just to see the new thing whole, and just because there were leaves, leaves and leaves out back, whole armfuls that you could use to build a house, scattered on the ground in what looked to be the garden, the dead garden of the white-board house that my uncle had said was the farmhouse of no farm but just a house on the road edge of a vineyard—a few acres of old vines, with a couple of three or four good bearers to put a piece of fruit on the table besides just grapes—lemon, pomegranate and loquat that my uncle said he was not so sure if he had a bush of or a tree of, but had anyhow enough of for this family, plenty for the table, plenty exotic enough for side-walkers from the city.

Artichoke is what they said the leaves were, artichoke is what the city people decided the leaves were the dead arms of, the dead-dragging dirt brooms that broke off loose from the piece of ground just behind the house that my aunt said was a whole table let go, a whole green table of God's earth given up to seed by who knows how many there were of the ones before, the people who let this whole place go for a bucket of plums, for what it took to gas up the Buick for a year, for table money.

I gathered up however many of the long, spidered-out-to-there dirt-sweepers I could wrap my arms around and put them around and up against the three or four wood crates I could find, belly-up or belly-down on the dirt or leaned up against the back side of the white-board house next to the three lizard-swept steps up to the door of the back porch—the backmost part of the house that stuck out like the short leg of an L, it looked to me—out toward the hardened path that came right up to the bottommost step and split the handful of what my uncle said was just enough acres to bury a small family of gophers, split the gopher haven acres in two, like a half-buried trunk of dead-fallen tree, fallen down long on its own hard grave.

· · ·

64

As my uncle dragged a burnt-gold-headed length of baked black hose to hook up to the spigot at the side of the house, I gathered up the long, spidered swatches of plant arms that my aunt said were artichoke, what else? What else so long and so leafed-out to the ground and planted in what looked like rows, green-garden rows enough not for a bachelor only but for a family of who knows how many, how many artichokes a big, healthy family could eat in a week, in a year, a who-knows-if-the-cow-don't way to put things that my aunt kept in her apron pocket for whenever it might come to a question of who, of what or of how many that concerned this particular family, a question put out on the table, for those times when there would be no cow anywhere in sight to put things straight.

While my uncle towed the spit-water black hose to the dirt around the lemon, the pomegranate and the loquat, I put up crates for corners and laid the leaves of artichokes against the wood boxes and up against each other, far enough away along the path trekked out from the white-board house to be alone under shade, so that I could look from the inside of a covered place both ways along what we were already calling the "split," the hardened dirt path trailed down the middle of the wide alley that cut a straight border between twin fields of vines from the back of the house to the edge of the new highway running the long back length of the whole property, the new, fast road to the city that the old farm road veered off from farther down in a Y-shape, the fast stretch that wrapped

a county arm around our vine-held acres row upon row, drap-
ing down to the ground of unpruned vines in the hollow of
the Y, with a footpath of boot-hard dirt, crossing the Y like
an H, road to road looked down, where who-knows-how-
many feet had booted out the wide, vine-dead distance, my
uncle said, just to see a fast car mow the green rows down,
going acres faster than what the black sign glinted, that anyone could see stuck down in tarred-up gravel just across the
road—glinting a flat, rounded five and a glinty-eyed O.

I kept enough stalks for walls and for a roof and left
a leaf window looking onto the white house and an open,
crawl-in space of a door, looking back toward the new highway that my uncle said had gone in permanent, and not for
just the we'll-see-how-she-goes kind of time that my uncle
was willing to give to most new things, things like an artichoke house in the middle of a vineyard or like a white just-
bought board house joint-ventured into with my father to see
how she goes all in due time, my uncle said, the kind of time
it took for things to settle down to good business and smell
like it, for a kitchen table to sit plumb to an elbow and for
glue-smelling linoleum to roll out right—that kind of we'll-
see kind of time. "Then but then we'll see about plow-fruit,"
is what my uncle told me, "about what's plow-fruit and
what's not."

Belly-down alone in the artichoke house, in spidery artichoke
shade, I could stick-shoot out of the crawl-in door at zoom

cars zooming somewhere past fifty, past the look-down double-barreled lane out of spider-leafed sight, stick-shot dead. And sometimes it wasn't a zoom car but just a pickupful of Mexicans standing up in the back of a gear-grinding truck, standing up to get shot with their hats on, their hands gripping the canopy rail and their knees buckling in the wind.

Spider-down low, I could turn around inside and spider-see out of the leaf window, see anything that moved under the draped vines or around the back of the white house. I could see my father and my uncle and my aunt pulling at things in the house-wide piece of ground where I had seen a house in the leaves, a house that the leaves could make. I could see my aunt with a hoe, my uncle with a rake, and my father with a shovel that looked to me like a shield that glinted sun off the back of it when my father would push the shovel into the ground and turn a piece of dirt over with it. I could see my aunt pulling with the hoe and my uncle raking toward my father in what looked to me like a circle toward the center— leaves, stalks, sticks, the dried-up things of the garden—pulling against the root-hold toward the center, like a slow spider pulling a jerky leg in.

When the things gathered in the center began to look to me like another bush in the garden, a high dead bush like a haystack, I spider-crawled out of my shade house and brushed small dirt clouds into the air, brushing my legs and my belly, breaking up clods of dirt under my rubber-soled shoes, stepping from one big clod onto another all the way back in toward the house just to look around and see how things were going to look now around the lemon, the pomegranate and the loquat, black glinty-eyed with shiny circles of laked-up water underneath and the trails of a spit-water snake running in the dirt from one watering hole to the next.

Boy-brother, I watched my sisters putting sticks at corners around the place where there were still a few stragglers, a few leaners, and still some green strawberries close-hung to the ground, and one of my sisters pulling the black neck of the hose over from the lake of the pomegranate, letting a sun-gold-headed length wave on its own now, full of the muscle that water makes in a hose, wave out across the mounded-up strawberries and then forcing the black neck down into the furrow river to drink.

Running in the dirt from one watering hole to the next with a boy-brother stolen length of water-stiff hose, I stuck the gold-rimmed head into one hole and then into the other of the ones holed-out together close under what my uncle said looked like a good bearer, a good treeful of cherry and a haven for gophers, a root haven for cherry root cut-and-pluggers down below. I stuck the snake head of hose in and ran the water down under, tunnel after tunnel, and pulled the water snake back out to look, to see who was running, who was running this haven and turning what inside out, God or a bunch of gophers, running mud mad, I thought, away from the flood—my thumb in the snake's mouth, making it hiss underneath, making the gophers foot it out in Y's and H's and clawed-out L's, I thought, in a whole alphabet of shapes dug crazy into dirt beyond, beyond cherry roots and our whole haven of a farm.

I stuck the snake head of the hose in one and then the other dark place where the small dirt piles made hills, and then I put my head down close to look, the water spilling away at the side, looking for one of the cut-and-pluggers to come out looking and get the snake with a thumb in its mouth, or to see some wet something crawl back down, crawl mud roads back, I thought, to kingdom come, or maybe just back to the next farm over.

Then my sister stopped the flood with a big-sister tug of the snake, reared up and spitting all the way back across the hardened path to spit around a few stuck-down sticks, and then lie down in dirt and make a river.

Hands off the berries, I watched my sister pull the string once and twice around whatever odd-found stick that could stand stick-tall to a few stragglers and a few blood-red leaners, fist-high above dirt-curving water, with raked and shield-plowed ground with straw stuck in it still, spread all around the small-rivered place where the strawberries were, looked to be the last fruit of, stick-fenced around in wet dirt, with still a stalk or two out loose of something to drag a boy-brother rake across, a slow-bouncing iron set of farmer's teeth, my uncle called them, with about another nickel's worth of something still left to chew.

I pulled my nickel's worth onto the pile in the middle, the few strands of broken-up frond and pulled-out root and curled leaf of something only the cow knows what, and watched my uncle pull out a blue-and-red box of stick matches from his shirt pocket and make his thumbnail make a stick-shot flame, and then I watched my uncle set the small, burning match against a ratchet leaf that burned slow for a while like a cigarette, and then arched down away from the flame, making a spiny ghost fan of what the leaf had been.

I watched the flame move along the leaves and stalks and start to wrap around the sides of the stack, sending up thin leaves of ash into the air, and I watched the pieces flutter and drift in the heat flow above the burning bush pile and then float out over to where the leaves were still green in the vineyard, and out over the place that my father and my uncle and my aunt had dug and raked and hoed, settling soft down onto the dirt clods and down among the low strawberries where my sisters were trying to fan the ash leaves falling away, catching the bigger pieces in their hands, as if they were catching butterflies, and just crumbling them up, instead of trying to save the wings.

We watched the pile in the middle of the garden burn stick-and-stem down, like a match-burnt, sun-spotted artichoke spider pulling all of its ratchet legs back in, and we watched my father swat the last things down with the shield-back of his shovel, and then pull the black neck of the hose over from the new islands of strawberries and make a shiny, wet cinder bush out of what was left.

Then I saw one of my sisters go to turn off the spigot at the side of the house and my father throw the black hose down to spit itself out, my uncle dragging the farmer's teeth across, chewing and spitting around wet cinder, and then my uncle bouncing the hard, flat head on the ground to clean the black iron teeth, and then just boot-bouncing the back of the iron head once or twice to get the last small bits off.

I took the flat iron rake from my uncle and head-bounced it over the hard path and over to the place at the side of the house where the spigot was, and I saw my father grab up both by the neck, the shovel and the hoe over to spigot-wash them clean, while my sisters wound the dead-looking, un-screwed muscle of the hose, two sisters wrapping it around the roots of a third sister-tree until the gold-rimmed head bounced up and the roots jumped out, away from the wet snake's mouth.

Watching my father spigot-wash the hoe, the shovel and the rake, I could see my aunt wiping her face with her apron and snapping off a few sun-split pomegranate bulbs from the bush, and then putting them into her apron, pulled up by one hand, those, and then a couple of sun-spotted little lemons from the tree in front of the back kitchen window, saying that the bird-pecked rest was all plow-fruit as far as this family was going to be concerned, and saying for us all to go wash up clean for some dinner come soon as she could scrape the dead out of a pot and get one back to life again.

Before we went in to wash, in the double-tubbed cement sink on the back porch, I held the wood slats up straight, the garage-found wood slats from a pile bound up with old string that my uncle said were for propping up down-drooping vines with, and my father and my uncle rolled a log of chicken wire around the place where the old garden was and where the strawberries drooped, blood red, from the wet dark mounds— the black-sooted, cinder-bush-buried piece of land that my uncle said it was a good thing to throw a weight of bones around before any more sun went down, just to get a few things settled in the dirt department as to what kind of green table this garden was going to be, all in good time—one under a new green thumb or one just under some black Mexican's, hat-faced, twice-blessed asleep under a nub-picked tree, like some bruised heap of God's exotic fruit.

Saving the Light

When my aunt said that God had put His dark palm over Old Pigeon George's eyes, my aunt sent us up the street, just after the operation, to the Fat Lady's gray-shingled big house with the giant pepper tree in front and Old Pigeon George's chicken-wire coops in back, just so Old Pigeon George could get used to hearing his way around the house and looking in at least the right direction, and be around a few friendly voices that he could put a face to for a summer afternoon, other than just house kin, and maybe even get a little braver about trying to find the toilet by himself if there were a few more friendly sounds around

that he could remember in that big house, and not have to just
sit by himself up in that front room all day on the couch,
swaddled up like some little kid with the blindfold still stuck
on after everybody else has gone home, listening to the flies
buzz at the screens and to the Fat Lady screaming at her fat
little daughter in the kitchen to swallow the Vicks out of the
blue jar or to down her cod-liver-oil spoonful before the Fat
Lady made her swallow the spoon too, not have to just sit
there, listening to the old pepper tree talk up a leaf storm,
crying out of the bottom of that bandage like an old baby,
my aunt said, waiting for God to chase all of those seed-steal-
ing blackbirds out of the sky.

I sat on the ottoman in the front room, while my sisters played
dolls with the Fat Lady's fat daughter in the bedroom or made
red Kool-Aid tea with the fat daughter's tin tea set in the kitch-
en, watching the Fat Lady take off what looked to me like a
white gauze wrapped-around blindfold, Scotch-taped onto
Old Pigeon George's forehead, and watching the Fat Lady
pull the white cotton puffs off of Old Pigeon George's
eyes and drop the wet puffs into the paper bag on the floor
full of used Kleenex, and then squeeze some drops out of
a bottle over each clouded-over eye that I could not see the
black dot of clearly, the way I could see the looking-back dots
in the Fat Lady's dark brown eyes, or the way it was easy to find
the red eye dot on the white-powdered jelly doughnuts that Old

Pigeon George would bring home to us from the bakery, the sprinkled-powdery-white puffs that I would first spit on the top of, and then rub the powder into a sticky white cloud over with my finger, licking the sticky cloud off then, and sucking out whatever red jelly I could out of the little red hole in the side before I would ever eat the puffy dead rest, because the dry white powder tickled too feathery on my tongue, me watching the clouded-over eyeballs twitch, looking somewhere up at the ceiling, I thought, while the tube spit little tears out of the pointy glass end and the water spilled out over Old Pigeon George's cheeks as if he was crying and just could not stop, I thought, as if the clouded-over eyes would not stop crying when someone took their little white stuck-on cotton clouds away.

I sat on the ottoman just to see if what they said was true, just to see what an eye looked like when you peeled the white powdery spots away so that the black dot in the middle could see right, and to hear if Old Pigeon George would maybe say that he could see right again, once somebody had taken the blindfold off, and did not need any more cotton or any more Kleenex or for somebody to walk him to the toilet, but could see at least the good enough to walk the few blocks with the red-tipped cane it took to get to the bakery or to just walk the dozen or so rickety gray wood steps down to the backyard and then just the little bit farther over the weed-gone patchy grass to the chicken-wire coops that had laying chickens and the kind of pigeons, raftered up on long sticks, who always came

75

home, living together in the same stick-and-wired-together coop up against the fence, with the red-feather-headed jerky-walk rooster, see maybe just the good enough to take me inside the curled-orange-and-gray-and-white-feather-crawled coop to feed the chickens and the pigeons and to maybe let me drag the green fan rake across the bird-dirtied dirt floor when it was time to change the straw around the hen-holed laying boxes and under the stick-raftered gray-and-white-feathered pigeons who flew in and flew out of the pigeon-size hole high up on the chicken-wired side of the coop, where there was what Old Pigeon George called his pigeon porch, the little flat piece of wood strutted out from under the hole in the bent-back wire, the black-dotted-red-eye pigeons that Old Pigeon George called his Daylight Savers, because the birds always came home before dark.

I sat on the ottoman and watched the Fat Lady put the fresh dry cotton puffs pulled out of the box that Old Pigeon George held on his lap over Old Pigeon George's watering eyes and then wrap the white gauze blindfold back around Old Pigeon George's gray-haired head, sticking a few pieces of Scotch tape onto his forehead and then down onto the white-wrapped bandage to keep the light tight out, the Fat Lady said, the light that was no good now on a sore eye needing a little rest from God and everybody, and needing the Venetian blinds pulled together a little closer than usual, so that what I was doing a little more than usual in that dark front room was listening while I was watching, just listening to the rip-and-stick-on sound of the Scotch tape and to the voice of a sister putting a make-believe crying doll to sleep in the bedroom or saying, "Tea's hot! Tea's hot!" in the kitchen to the fat little daughter, and listening to the flies buzzing on the window screens and to the voice of the Mexican, coming from the downstairs stoop across the street, the Mexican who would sit out and play the guitar to nobody special most every afternoon when you could see the wrecked truck parked out in front, singing what the Fat Lady said was the one about the sky, his voice floating in the air from across the street and coming through the summer-screened and Venetian-blinded windows, even with the leaf storm that the pepper tree made, trying to rub those little red things off against the screens, singing my most favorite one after the one about the cockroach, the song about the pretty little blue sky, and someone singing his sighs up to his sweetheart to come out to look at the little blue sky from her window.

When the Fat Lady said that maybe it was better for me to go play out on the teeter-totter and not watch anymore just then when Old Pigeon George said that he had to go down the hall for a little bit to use the necessary and did not want anybody to watch, I turned back again from outside the back-porch door and watched the Fat Lady take Old Pigeon George by the arm and walk him into the dark hallway and then push in the door of the toilet so that I could see a door-frameful of white

77

tile-boxed light blink open into the dark front room and then blink back again closed like a giant shut blind.

I sat on the teeter-totter alone because no one of my sisters and not even the little fat girl wanted to teeter-totter just right then and I watched the little black birds and the other just ordinary-looking birds that were free and not cooped up anywhere fly right up to the bird cages pegged up the whole side of the big gray house, the bird cages with the little ordinary-looking everyday birds jailed up in them that the Fat Lady's husband had caught in the backyard, they told me, and kept cooped up just because he liked to keep things, and take care of them and give them a roof out of the storm, watched the other birds fly right up to the wire-and-stick cages hung off of wood pegs jutted out from the side of the house, and reach in with their beaks to take the seed from their brothers, I thought, right out of the little wooden boxes, and then fly back off to a tree in the backyard or up into nowhere quicker than I could look. And I could still hear the voice of the Mexican singing, coming from across the street and floating up the driveway over to where I was in the long patchy grass backyard with just a big long whisker-splintery board laid over a cement-filled oil barrel painted green for a teeter-totter, something that I could play blindman on the bridge on when nobody else would come out and sit down on the other side, play blindman on the bridge on when I took off my T-shirt and tied it around my head so that I could just see my toes when I looked down and walked the whole way over the bridge without falling off or having to see any more than just my toes, and saying that I was another blindman, different from the one who had gone before, whenever I did fall off, mostly on purpose, getting more grass stains on my pants than my aunt said it was all right for me to get, falling off mostly when the long-bonking board would start to tilt over to come down on the other side with a ground bonk that would send a million splinters up my spine, depending on where on the board I stood, and sometimes even make me bite my tongue not anyhow on purpose if it landed before I was ready, tilting slowly and then faster over the world to the other side, when the blindman was supposed to run faster than a bridge could fall, a bridge caught on fire and falling in long burning splinters down to hell rocks and rivers down below.

I played blindman on the bridge until I said all of my blindmen were dead in the water, or dead on hell rocks, and I called for a sister to please come out and not even have to be anybody but have to just sit down on the everyday-ordinary other side of the splintery-board teeter-totter and go ditch-down low on her side so that I could go up into hand-splintered, breath-stopped nowhere, like the birds, and come back down into everything just home, but no sister would put the doll or the teacup down just then when I called, so that I just walked like an everyday-ordinary man, with my hands in my pockets and not anywhere out for balance, walked and did not run like a blindman running from the world on fire, but walked with my T-shirt back on like a sidewalk man, over what I said was just a steep hill, to throw gravel bits at the rooster or to see if I could spot an egg through a hen hole, and what I spotted instead was just a dead one down on the feather-curled dirt floor of the coop, one of the gray-and-white-feathered ones that Old Pigeon George said were his Daylight Savers, with just something white coming out of the little hole where a dotted red eye had been, that had been maybe pecked out by the rooster or pecked out by even one of his brothers, and that would maybe be better off cooped up in the garbage can than down there where there was more than just feathers flying when one or two of those Daylight Savers were not in any light-saving mood, Old Pigeon George would say, more scuttling across that dirt floor than just that dumb rooster, trying to peck the wishbone out of some poor hen's back.

And I looked at all the places down around the fence-board back of the coop that I thought looked dark enough and that looked to me like something that a rat would call a door, where the wood was chipped off to a chewed-looking angle or splintered up with wet rot from the bottom into a set of ragged wood teeth, places I thought might be just big enough to drag a dead feathered thing into, and I threw bits of gravel at the white-eyed, stiff-footed dead-fallen bird, trying to get the bits of gravel to maybe hit on the little white hole, and then I just threw the rest of what I had just anywhere on the thing that I said was too dumb or too weak to even save itself against a brother, or to stretch a wing over a red- and black-dotted speck of world, I thought, when it was time to fight or to fly to somewhere safe, and not just fall off like a blindman off a burning bridge into water or onto hell rocks or onto what I said was even worse—onto the ditch-dead bottom of the world, onto all the sky-fallen feathers and the dirty, trickled-down straw.

I walked a last ordinary-man walk over the teeter-totter and threw a few bits of gravel at the little blackbirds hooked up onto the wire sides of the little roofed bird cages pegged up under the wide, wood-beam and shingle-overhung roof of the big gray house, the blackbirds stealing from their brothers' houses, I thought, a peck at a time through the square-wired little windows, and then I walked down the gravel driveway to the gray-staired stoop out front under the pepper tree so that I could watch the Mexican, singing and playing the guitar across the street, and throw the little red-pepper balls at the cars passing, all the little red-pepper balls that just fell down from the wind or that the tree grated against the green-shingled roof of the big gray house and against the summer-screened windows down into a red-berry ocean all around the tree over the weed-gone grass and across the cement walk, little hard red berry balls that I could step on and crush or throw at the wheels of cars going by and still have a million little red berry balls left, the whole while I waited for the Fat Lady's husband to drive his long gray pipe-winged pickup truck into the gravel driveway under the pepper tree, me going up the stairs to ring the doorbell the once or twice until the Fat Lady told me to just stop, me saying my hello through the screen door to Old Pigeon George, just sitting on the fuzzy brown couch, alone in the dark front room, like the one who has to stay and count to a hundred while everybody else gets to go and hide, me just waiting then, on the steps, until the pickup truck with the long gray pipes laid into metal hooks along the sides of the truck turned into the gravel driveway, when the Fat Lady's husband, who always had a cigarette hanging down at the corner of his mouth, bounced the butt of his hand on the horn before he got out of the truck and walked me back to the long patchy grass yard behind the big gray house, where we could still hear the Mexican singing and playing the guitar from the downstairs stoop across the street, and where the Fat Lady's husband pulled the little roofed cages down, one by one, with his hook pole, standing up on the ladder, and let me pour the seeds out of the bag from the basement out into the little feed boxes of just the everyday-ordinary birds fluttering around inside, and where the Fat Lady's husband then took each little roofed cage house and poled it up onto the right peg, while the ash dropped from the end of his cigarette and dusted down onto the patchy, weed-gone grass underneath.

82

. . .

I stood on the cement-barrel middle of the teeter-totter, doing my blindman-seeing-again-balance from one long-tilting side to the other, while the Fat Lady's husband walked inside through the wood-boxed-in wire pull-door of the coop, and picked up the dead bird by the red stick feet, dropping little red-sparked ashes that turned to just gray down the front of his khaki shirt, and I called for just any one of my sisters to please come out onto the gray wood porch outside of the back kitchen door for only a minute and to just look before it might be too late and they might maybe be all back in by then, the last few fat stragglers, flying down out of the sun-falling-down nowhere of sky over the patchy grass backyard, down to the sticked-out piece of wood off the side of the chicken-wire coop that Old Pigeon George called his pigeon porch, to go in, and go in, through the bent-back wire hole, and step sideways, one red lifted skinny bird foot after the other, out onto all that mattered, the Fat Lady's husband said, out onto some bird-known-only place on that long stick, to clamp a firm, homecoming foot and to close a small light-saving lid, skintight down on this dark-roofed, light-stealing big blind ball of a world.

The Hunter, the

Chinaman and the

Man out of Africa

The Saturday when my sisters said I had stayed in bed ten years past breakfast, when my sisters had already had the two-ton iron skillet soaking in the sink and the cold, rubbery, burnt last-took hotcakes already dumped over the wet coffee grounds in the newspaper-lined garbage can in the pantry, my father said for my sisters to cook me up an egg or two and a cut of bacon so that I could get a little piece of food in me sometime before dinner, and so that he would not have to dig any more good money out of the black ditch other men could call a pocket, and have to drag one son hungry through the whole damn seeing neighborhood up to the stores on Fourteenth, looking for some lard-dipped damn diner or other and have to go in and pay not even white nor kin, but a man out of Africa, to drop a two-bit white egg on a lard-slicked burnt black griddle, and charge a fellow workingman, a man looking into the same black pit every day that he was, a lousy extra ditch-dug dollar.

My sisters said it was about ten years too late and a big too bad that I did not get up and eat when it was nice and hot, and for my father and me to get out of the way of what was going to happen now to this kitchen under new management, the mop and scrub this kitchen was going to get without any orders from my aunt upstairs anymore, without anybody else saying where the pots went in the pantry and how many carrots to cut up for the stew, and just how high to nail the black mammy-woman in the red bandanna and the bald black butler-man with the curly white hair going around the ears, each biting into a wedge of watermelon, painted plaster potholder hooks, higher or lower up on the wall, because they, my sisters, were going to bring things up to date and scrub that woman upstairs right off of this family's back, starting right there in that kitchen, starting right under our feet, and that they would be cooking up the dinner from now on at six o'clock sharp, and not my aunt anymore, coming down to stick her nose in the pot, and that they would be putting breakfast on the table weekends when called, and for my father and me to go chase a hen hell-to-hot-water-and-back someplace else out of the way of the mop, unless we were planning to get a Spic and Span shoeshine or to step into the pantry to sling up the garbage can on our way out.

My father said that he would rather wake up and be a chicken in a pot than wake up in a house where a man had to fight to put a piece of food on a kid's plate and for me to stretch an eye open big as an egg that we were going right up to Fourteenth Street to get, right up to those stores and to look in every damn window as well, and maybe even get something special for winter to slip an arm into, so that he did not have to go to work and so that I did not have to go to school, both starved out of the house and naked to the wind.

After I had fast-walked the couple of door-slammed-behind blocks up to Fourteenth Street with my father, and after my father had said that the skinny-between-stores, red-stooled luncheonette with the little green awning smelled just like the right business, my father sat with a cup of coffee while I poked holes into the yellow eyes of my two eggs and pulled the red strings off of my strips of bacon, saying that the yellow eyes were too runny and that the white part on the bacon was just too blubbery for me to eat, while the colored man in the white paper soldier-flap cap scraped his flipper across the griddle and pushed the extra little white and yellow bits and the run-out

86

grease from the bacon into a black groove running all around the sides of the griddle, and my father told me then to eat every last little crumb of white bread toast with the yellow melting eyes of butter on it, every crumb on the plate with the little green arrows going around the edge, before he threw the whole damn mess through the window that my father then told the colored man could use a little extra wipe with a loose rag, and the colored man then told my father that he was only the cook and only fried them up and did not write the price of any white egg in the house, and my father said then that he would just as soon be robbed by a man with a gun than by a fellow workingman who ought to know the worth of a dollar, robbed down to the hole in his shoe rather than have to sit there and pay more for just two than for a whole damn dozen, two eggs that ought to be served at least in a bowl the next time, so that a man would not have to grease up his soles and run like a chicken after eggs slid halfway back to the henhouse on his store-day off. Then my father pulled his cowboy curlicued leather wallet from his back pocket and fingered out one dollar and then another and put the bills down onto the counter, and then the colored man counted out the change back down onto the shiny red counter, the change that my father usually let me keep for gum or to put in my world bank, and then my father just pushed the little pile of gum money or candy money or world-bank money under the milky-white plate with the little green arrows going around the edge and with the round puddle of black coffee moated around his cup, and said "Thank you" to the colored man, "Thank you for feeding us two gentlemen up."

I walked with my father along the storefronts on Fourteenth Street, sucking the little powdery-white candy with the green gummy dot inside that came from the small bowl by the cash register in the diner, past the yellowed window with the gray cartons of eggs stacked up inside behind the red-and-white writing that said BREAKFAST ANYTIME, and past the store-front right next door with the pictures of babies stood up on flapped-back cardboard stands in the window, past all the stores to the end of the block where the blue sign said GOOD-WILL on it, with baby cribs and mattresses and ski poles jammed together in the same room in the window, until we got to the toggery a couple of blocks farther, the store that had the gum-eraser-colored, no-faced men chrome-poled in the windows, wearing the red-and-black-checkered, flap-down-eared hunting caps, and dungarees stretched out empty on wires that we could see in the front part of the windows, with orange and brown curled leaves sprinkled all over the pants that looked to me like they were running away scared from the no-faced hunters, the way I would run the last part of the way under the trees, always late to school.

My father took my hand then and pushed us through the swing door of the toggery that had the picture of the big gorilla up giant on the wall, on past the rows of stacked-up dungarees to where my father said the empty sleeves were just hanging around waiting for two men just about our size to go on over and slip an arm through something that would keep them both from being naked to the wind that winter, and I put my arms through the sleeve holes of the yellow wool plaid coat that I liked that the man with the little mustache held out for me to try on while my father put on the long black, bent-metal-hook-hooked raincoat that my father said would be good to keep a little weather off of his back when the rainy season came, and then my father said that maybe the man with the little mustache would not mind so much throwing in one of the beanie-boy caps stacked up in a pile over by the cash register, throwing in one of those beanie-boy caps with the shiny-mirror cutout stars and cutout diamonds and little colored charms sewn onto the pie-wedged top part, and with the edge of the flipped-up flap going around like a sailor cap, saw-toothed like the teeth on a pumpkin, that maybe the man would not mind throwing a beanie-boy cap in for a kid with a sick mother in the hospital, a mother, you know, my father said to the man with the little mustache, a little sick and having a hard time, that maybe the man with the little mustache would not mind taking off a few dollars for a workingman with a kid trying to do the best he could, and then the man with the little mustache said that the beanie-boy cap was only three dollars, and I said then that it was all right if I did not get the hat, but my father said that he thought it would be a nice thing if the man with the little mustache would take a few dollars off for a fellow workingman and make a kid happy and the man with the little mustache reached up then, and took the wine-colored cap that the man said was my favorite color, wasn't it? the first one right on top of the pile, and put it onto my head, saying to my father that business was business and that everybody he knew was a workingman, including himself, and that some other things just were not good business, not the way he was taught to do business at all. Then my father reached back and pulled out his cowboy curlicued wallet and counted out the money and then gave me the change to pocket, and said "Thank you" to the man with the little mustache and told me to say a thank-you to the man for giving me the nice present with all the mirror cutout stars and diamonds and the little Chinaman tassel dangling off the top, and then my father pushed us out of the swing door of the toggery, me in my new yellow wool plaid coat that my father said made me look like a real hunter, and with the wine-colored beanie-boy cap on my head that my father said made me look like a real Chinaman, and my father wearing the long black, bent-metal-hook-hooked raincoat, because he had told the man with the little mustache that he hated to see the sleeves folded up in a bag, the long black raincoat that I said to my father made him look like a fireman, just walking around on his Saturday day off from the fire.

. . .

I walked with my father past the Saturday-open stores along Fourteenth Street that my father went to on his store-day off to get a roast for the week, or to just look in the window the way we did at the Red Goose shoe store, looking at all the shoes stood together in pairs that I said were for red men and brown men and black men and that my father said would have to wait in the window a little while longer, until the shoes he had on wore out, and I carried the white waxed bag from the store that had pans of potato salad and macaroni salad with sliced-open olive eyes crisscrossed over the mounds behind the slant glass counter, and that had all the sliced salami and the square pieces of white cheese and orange-colored cheese and the slices of the kind of bologna with the white dots in it, and the square slices wrapped up of the kind of meat that my father liked in his lunch that looked to me like bits of tongue frozen in no-colored Jell-O, all the slices wrapped up in the cloudy white waxed paper that my aunt used to put up the lunches for the week, and my father carried the big brown bags, one under each black-raincoated arm, past the dress-up store so that my father could look at the hats on the no-faced wooden men, until we got to the block where we had to cross the street where there was no stoplight, and I walked on the side of my father that was away from the cars coming, switching sides in the middle of the street until we got to the other side, where I always jumped the curb, and where you could see the little green wooden shack of the colored man who shined shoes at the end of a row of stores next to the gravel driveway, the little green wooden cabin with the one window in the front where my father always went on his store-day off to get a shine put on his crack-lined black leather shoes for the Sunday in church, and I sat up next to my father on the old car seat in the tiny one-man house with the slippery iron foot things pronged up to stand your shoes on to get the shine, with one big brown bag next to me on the seat and the little white waxed bag piled up on top of the other big brown bag on my lap, and I looked at all of the pictures of the naked women on all of the walls and on the ceiling of the little hut, naked women on beaches with green palm trees, pointing their toes in the sand, and naked women sitting on bar stools, one of them holding a skinny V-shaped glass and biting the stemmed cherry that I had seen the corner bartender, who gave me sodas and my uncle little shots of whiskey, drop red-floating down to the bottom of a glass, and naked women lying down on what looked to me like sharp, jagged rocks, with blond hair blowing in the wind, naked women that looked to me like they were real and not just pictures, but real women who somehow all knew each other, all looking at me sitting on the car seat with the bags, next to my father, and looking at my father, pulling out his white handkerchief from his back pocket and wiping the sweat off of his forehead from doing all the walking in the big black raincoat with the metal hooks sprung jangly-open, and from carrying the heavy

brown bags, naked women looking their always-at-you, sideways and straight-across and even straight-down-looking look
from their other, all-alone-naked-woman rooms and from sky-
blue places all over the world, looking at the back of the bald-
headed colored man with the curly white hair around his ears,
naked women with white-skinned, pink-nippled titties smiling
from the pictures pasted flat on the walls and on the ceiling,
looking at me and at my father and at the colored man as if
we were the naked ones, I thought, the colored man patting on
the black paste out of the can with just slaps of his bare fingers,
all the way around on my father's shoes, while my father asked
the colored man how business was, the colored man saying
back that business was always stepping up, doing the big
whiskery brush in swooshes across and alongside, and then
putting the little white puddles on the toe caps with the
bottle-dipped fuzz ball of white world stuck on a pin, it looked
to me, the size of a drink-dropped cherry, and then spreading
each white puddle until it disappeared under the rag with a
few shimmy pulls down and across that I always looked to
catch the quicker-than-I-could-see back-snap of, my father's feet
slipping off of the shiny iron, pronged-up shoe stands, kid-small
to the sole of my father's shoe, the way my feet would always
slip off of my youngest sister's feet when we would roll down
on our backs on the carpet and put the bottoms of our shoes up
together to touch and say then that we were married, and then
try to push each other off of the bridge or mountain or off of
the world, saying that we each wanted a divorce now, my

father's feet slipping off of the shiny iron kid-size stands every few snaps or so as if my father was trying to step down, it looked to me, onto some missed stair or missed rung of a ladder or still-spinning bicycle pedal, and trying, with his foot pumping the air, to touch a stair underneath, or to catch the rung or the spinning pedal, trying to climb down from where he was or trying just to match his step again to what he had married.

When the colored man took the prong thing out of its socket for my father to step down past all the brushes and the bottles and the shoe-wax cans, I watched my father reach into his pocket to pay the colored man and then have to reach back and get out his cowboy curlicued wallet and give the man the dollar instead of the coin, and then I heard my father say to the colored man for him to keep a quarter for himself and to give the quarter left over to the little Chinaman bringing home all the bacon these days, days getting on over to the lean side, and then the colored man put the quarter out of his cigar box into my hand and closed back the lid and told my father not to worry about any old rain cracking through one of his shines, and that the weatherman had told him that morning private that we were all fixed up most certain to have a nice long day of sun.

I walked with my father then, the few blocks home, my father carrying the big brown bags, one under each arm, and me just carrying the white waxed paper bag packed with enough peel-off slices for a week, so that it was easy for me to jump when a curb came up, my father making a jiggling sound that I could hear whenever my father put a wax-cracking foot down, me walking my beanie-boy, one-bag circles around my father, watching the sweat run down out of his hat onto his forehead and around by his ears, and I opened the back-porch door for my father after making all the beanie-boy circles I could make going up the driveway, and followed my father the one step up inside, and then my aunt, that I could see crying and knocking and pulling at the doorknob of the locked inside door to where we lived downstairs, said to my father, as we both stepped up inside the porch, for my father to open his eyes for once to see whether it was raining or shining all day long on his doorstep under her kind roof, and to go in, if he could find the key to open the door, and see what was burning her heart to a cinder in that oven in there that was not the chicken that she had made, all floured up and ready on the platter for her to come down and fry in the big black kettle, the chicken that was going to be for whom now exactly if it was not going to be for the all of us that she double-cooked-and-cleaned for, just to get a slammed door in the face, and then my father put down the big brown bags on the porch bench and took off the black bent-metal-hook-hooked raincoat and pinched off his cream-colored straw hat and hung the long coat and the hat up on a couple of the twist-wire screwed-in coat hooks on the wall behind the porch door, and then my father took out his white handkerchief from his back pocket and wiped at his forehead, and my aunt asked who then was going to put out that fire in her house, burning her heart up to a cinder, if the fireman did not, if the fireman was out getting a shimmy-sport shoeshine and dressing up his kid with a bunch of bitty mirrors and beads and jigglies on his head like a man out of Africa, and then my father said for me to take off my new yellow wool coat and to take off my beanie-boy cap and to leave them for just a little while down on the round oak table on the porch, and said for me to go upstairs then, and have a little piece of chicken with my aunt and with my uncle for just to be nice, and for me maybe to come back down in a little nice while when all this fire down below was good and out and scraped into a ditch that he was going to tend to in another minute, and that he would come to the bottom of the stairs and call me down himself when it was just that time for every two-bit man out of Africa to come and sit down at his own table with his own family and see what this new God they had had scraped down into his own damned sweet black-burnt Almighty-heavy pot.

Dressing Up

for the War

My father kept a long, silky pink nightgown in a drawer for my mother to wear when she came home, a nightgown that my aunt said was wrong to keep with a man's things and useless to waste a whole big drawer on, a whole dresser drawer on flimsy-flung nothing, laid out snake-naked at the bottom to a waste of good space, a nightgown that lasted in the drawer for about as long as the old rags lasted in the box in the hall closet that my aunt cut and tore every new-bought nightgown into, saying that polishing the dining-room table was twice the more useful than keeping an empty frill, pink in a man's drawer, in a man's chest of things, with no woman home to wear it about a small house full of young children, thanks be to God, and that it was better worn out to good purpose on the something-to-be-proud-of legs of a table that company could see when company came over, than worn out on the hollow, wish-broken bone of a stubborn man's mind.

The times when the drawer was empty and the rag box in the hall closet was full of yellowed old pillowcases and pieces of undershirt, and full of the silky pink strips that my aunt made out of any nightgown that she said had lain out snake-naked long enough to be put to some real use around the house, my father would send my oldest sister to the ladies' store up on Fourteenth Street that had ladies' panties push-tacked up the walls in the front windows, and black and white and pink brassieres stretched across pink-powder-puff-colored, no-headed and no-armed plaster bust shapes of women, and maybe a white or light blue or light rose-colored silky robe, dressed on the tall, pink-powder-puff-colored model-woman, standing with one plaster knee bending out from between the flaps of the robe in the ladies' store that we always passed by while going to get the groceries, standing with her arms stretched out at her sides and her fingers pointing outward the way girls in skirts held out their hands when a wind came up, I thought, the model-woman with curly plaster grooves of hair painted yellow, and lips painted red, smiled around a mouthful of white plaster teeth, and who had little pumpkins hanging on strings from

her fingers at Halloween, and little shiny, wire-looped colored
Christmas tree bulbs hanging from her fingers at Christmas,
and red hearts for Valentine's Day, smiling the white smile in
the window of the store that my father said was no place for a
man to get his pipe filled, but a place where a big girl who
looked a little older might maybe find the right something a
mother might want to come home to sometime and curl right
up cozy to sleep in.

On the Saturday when my oldest sister had gone up to Fourteenth Street with the twenty-dollar bill from my father, my
middle sister stood up on a kitchen chair to clean the windows,
spraying from the blue bottle and rubbing the glass until we
could all hear the glass squeak, while my youngest sister and I
rubbed the legs of the dining-room chairs and the knob-carved,
stumpy spool legs of the dining-room table with the lemon-
oiled pieces of pillowcase or the torn undershirt rags, going
back after the oil had dried a bit to shimmy-shine the knobby
joints of the stump legs with the pink strips of silky cloth that
my aunt said polished up a good welcome, the silky pink strips
that we called shimmy dresses when we went back and forth
across the wood faces and the wood titties and the round wood
hips and the stumpy, knee-boned legs of the dining-room table,
shimmy dresses on the women and silk neckties on the men,
and sometimes I would do the woman doing her shimmy, and
sometimes I would just be the man doing my silk necktie, and

then doing my belt, and then just shining up my shoes while my sister did the shimmy slow, and then the shimmy medium, and then the shimmy last-dance-fast until the silky rag snapped off and her woman was naked, and my man was all dressed up to go to war.

That Saturday when my two other sisters and I had gotten to putting the paste wax down onto the linoleum floor with the old sheet, shirt and pillowcase rags, going square to square over the brick-colored tile floor that covered the downstairs, when the Venetian blinds had been dropped back down and you could still make a snake slide with your finger over the oily top of the dining-room table, my oldest sister showed us the thing she had shown my father, out working in the garden, the silky pink thing wrapped in the white crinkly tissue paper, with skinny pink straps and snow-flaky, cream-colored lace going around the top, opening up the ladies' store bag in the bedroom where my sisters all three slept so that my aunt coming down the stairs to empty the garbage pail or to check up on the housecleaning would not see the new one right away and maybe would not even think to look in the empty drawer in my father's room for a nice long time, my oldest sister opening up the ladies' store bag and spreading out the new nightgown over the nubbly rivered white bedspread on top of the iron bed, and then closing the bedroom door and going into the closet to take off her dress and to put the new nightgown on, the silky-pink shimmy dress that my oldest sister stood up on her toes between the pulled-back wire- and wood-hangered clothes to show us all how it would look on a woman who my oldest sister said was not that much bigger anyplace than she was getting to be, no place that much bigger but tall.

While my sisters had their drawers all pulled out in the back bedroom, folding and refolding their clothes and rolling their socks up together, waiting for the paste wax out of the yellow can to dry dull all over the downstairs tiled linoleum while my sisters did their drawers over and put on wool socks to slide down the hall in later when the floor would be shimmy-shined smooth and slippery, I closed the door of the bedroom where I slept in the bed with my father, and took off my dungarees with the blue elastic suspenders always clamped on, and then took off my snap-buttoned cowboy shirt and pulled the silky pink nightgown, which my oldest sister had folded down into the crinkly white paper-lined drawer, over my head and over my white T-shirt and then down over my legs, knobbing my knees up inside so that I could feel the shimmy-shiny on my skin, going bony knee up and then bony knee down on the little knotted-braid carpet down by the bed, trying to see myself in the shiny glass face of the alarm clock on the bed stand, trying to see myself in the yellow-shade-pulled-down room, while my aunt did her all of a sudden quick-walk tiptoe up a wax-spread hallway to check up on the clean and polish, opening the bedroom door still balanced up off of her heels, with me just standing on the little braid carpet, tiptoed up in my black-and-white canvas high tops, dressed in the silky pink shimmy dress from the ladies' store, my aunt then pulling at the silky pink I said I only wanted to feel on my skin the way my sisters said they could always feel their legs in dresses, feel the wind rushing up their legs cold, pulling at the pink thing that I was trying then to pull back over my head, ripping sideways and longways until she had the silky thing all off of me and in her hands and then walking back down the circle-streaked, drying hallway to the back bedroom and ripping the silky rest of the nightgown into rag strips in front of my sisters, saying that she would put the snake back into the box where it belonged, into the cardboard box in the hall closet with all of the rest of the crazy things that slithered out of that stubborn man's mind.

My sisters hid little bit pieces rolled up with their socks and I tore off a little strip from a corner that looked to me like just another pink piece of the world, and I dropped the silky pink strip into the dark slot of my world bank that opened at the bottom, where there was only blue and white, my world bank that I shimmy-shook the pennies and the nickels and the quarters and the big half-dollars inside of until I could say that all of Africa and all of South America and all of Australia were rich to the top, and that I was at least as rich as the bottom of

the pink Dominion of Canada, when I would open up the
slot cap at the bottom of the tilted world with a penny, and
shimmy-shake out what I had saved up so far for my father
to put in a real bank, always putting back inside the little silky
piece of cloth that slid out with the coins, the way we always threw the rags back into the box when we had finished
hands-and-knees rubbing in a circley shine, quick so that we
could go and slide on the new wax in our socks, threw the rags
down toward that corner where they would sometimes catch
on the edge of the box that my aunt said was no proper hook
for a smudged piece of filth, so that you would have to kick
the box with your toe to make the rags go back in right, one
always managing to hang back at the rim the while you had to
watch to make sure that something was moving down there,
sliding back in on its own, or before you had to step into the
dark closet and give the cardboard box a little kick, and watch
the piece that you had taken, the part that had either won or
lost the war, slip back inside into some shimmy-slid, flung
snake of a fold.

The Last

Man on Earth

My aunt would say that my sisters were three wills willed of the same bent willow, mad-bent against the world like their mother, against God and a good person's reason, a switch broom of wild hair in place of a straight answer that my sisters were but leaf and stem of, with the same hang of wild knots strung together to make a Jesus weep, and that we would all see whose branch would break first and willow-weep most when my father's face was the one to snap back to, and that the twig switch set on top of the refrigerator was just that reminder, a needle pointing in the direction that these things were going to take, whatever things they were that time that my sisters had said or done to bend her branch the wrong way to the side of commotion for young girls ever to take upon themselves in the face of a provider, to take up into their smart heads and out onto their switch-forgetful tongues, like a quiver of arrows sent switching against her, instead of just doing the thing said, the thing least expected in return to the provider, the sweeping of the home place clean, or maybe if not the iron, then the fold-and-put-away, stacked-up even of the clothes of the man who brings home the dinner and the flapped-back shut of the ironing board into the wall on the porch, as asked, as a least thing expected, instead of a switch broom tossed back in the very rooms provided, by some one or other of my sisters, like a self-willed wicked standing willow, bent on splitting wild hairs against any brisk wind and God.

Whenever the twig switch on top of the refrigerator upstairs was somehow bent the wrong way to the side of commotion, with the pointy end sticking out over the cake cover, or whenever my aunt found the switch in the toilet bowl, broken up into a handful of stick fingers that would not flush, we would watch my aunt get my uncle's wood-handled wing shears from the garage and snap down another twig from one of the fruit trees, just in case the first switch broke, so that my aunt could always go back and get the twin brother, we thought, or maybe snap the one this time shot out the little greener and likelier to bend, not break, into nubbed stick fingers for my aunt to wet-pinch out of the bowl of the toilet.

From the porch window or from behind the low, big-iron-bed bedroom window, we would watch my aunt walk under the fruit trees with the long-handled shears, looking for a branch that was the right thin enough and long enough for three girls to live with and a young tree to live without, we thought, going back and forth under the trees until she found the one it would be nothing to cry about to cut, and my sisters would then say that my aunt had her black finger right back on top of everything, just waiting to point at the who-to-blame-most.

When my aunt had the new black finger up on top of the cake cover with a "We'll see how the bough bends," or the maybe two fingers up there that time, together, like the big and little hands of a cake-cover clock, both skinny points pointing to the same, somewhere-out-there unlucky number, my sisters would send me up into the kitchen upstairs where my aunt lived, to see how long what was up there was, how pointy-out over the refrigerator, and to see if my aunt had left any of the hard nubs on.

I would then climb up onto the plastic-covered kitchen chair nearest the refrigerator to look and maybe even to touch for my sisters, and my aunt would tell me it would be best for me to just stay out of this wind entirely, out of the direction this wind was going to take tonight when my father would come home to put a few stray arrows back into their proper quiver.

In the time before my father came home, the long waiting time before dinner, I would tell my sisters what I could tell from just only having to look and guess and having to stay my stay-away-entirely, and my sisters would do the things that they said were things you could do to keep that black finger at a distance and keep the nubs from cutting in in places that things, my sisters would always tell me, were not supposed ever to touch the anywhere-near-the-nub part of on a girl, or on any woman either.

In that time, I would go into the bedroom and watch my sisters put on more panties than just their one pair, and then pull on the bottoms to their fluffy, wishing-wells-and-buckets pajamas, then roll the wishing wells and buckets all up their legs and under their skirts and put on the kind of sweater that buttons up in front, and then my sisters would send me to the bottom drawer of the dresser in my father's little double-bedded room, with the tied-back gauze curtains and the yellow shade always half down, to get the thick wool work socks, rolled up into what looked to me like fists, pushed down tight in two straight rows between a few skinny-over-the-shoulder thin undershirts and some old man's kind of long underwear, stacked up neat as pancakes to the corners. And I would walk back down the hallway with fist-lumps under my shirt, shots to the ribs and to the belly and maybe one under the belt, and I would just go in and lie down for the count on the big white bedspread and let my sisters take all the lumps, all the fists to unroll and push down flat in front underneath where it might just go, my big sister would say, where it had gone before a few times and might go again. Then my sisters would sit down on the big iron bed and put the wool socks down so that they would be just down right over any nub part, so that I would be the one to have to stand up and say what it all looked like under a sweater buttoned all the way up to the top. Then my sisters would tell me to close the door behind and just go and stay away someplace until dinner and after dinner and maybe even after that, until I got to be a girl myself sometime and had to stay and wait all day on the bed for my father.

I did my stay away where I could be on the porch to see my father when he walked by the windows and stood big in the doorway of the back garage that was the washroom for the clothes and a place for a man to come home to get the dirt off of himself first, in some way decent before dinner, my father would say, dirt that was all on him and on his boots, where I could see from to tell my sisters when my father had come home from work, and where it was all right for me to play last man at the fort, the two-stepped-up landing of the stairs, behind the iron-grille gate off the back of the porch room, where the rose-carpeted rest of the clunk-sounding steps went what we always said were eighteen wrong ways up to my aunt.

It was all right to be the man at the gate so long as I was not the man in the way whenever my aunt went up or down and so long as I did not draw back the black iron pull thing that opened the licorice-twist grille gate to the fort and let it go with a bing that you could hear all over the house. Or I could be the last man at the fort alive to hear the one-single-one that I would only ever want to listen to, the one that my aunt would put for me up on top of the no-good needle, wood stand-up Victrola on the porch, the porch being what my aunt said was the only room right for a wood stand-up Victrola in any house anywhere to be stood up in, if I would just only ask and let my aunt do the what-she-knew-the-how part and if I would do the stay-there-and-listen-good part, like the white dog stuck on the inside propped-up wood cover of the stand-up Victrola, the stay-there-and-listen-good part to the one that was the Combined Choirs of St. Vladimir's and St. Nikodim's that was my one-single-one that I liked, until it was the scratches-at-the-end time to go knock on the door of the bedroom and ask if any one sister would come out just only for a minute and turn the record over or please to take the no-good needle off. I listened to the one that was the Combined Choirs of St. Vladimir's and St. Nikodim's black-scratched record until no one of my sisters would come out anymore to do the needle back, but only would come out to push the finger handle up to OFF and then go back into the bedroom and close the door, so that I just did the last man at the fort with the back and forth of the iron-grille gate and sometimes a little bing when the pull thing slipped off my finger until I could hear my father's lunch pail making another metal sound in the driveway and until I could see my father moving his little side-to-side moving when even he was walking straight, me seeing through the porch-door window—my father, not looking back or even in, but walking from side to side a little until he was big in the out-back doorway of the washroom, and then big like a boxer with his arms stretched out, taking off his green-faded army coat and sitting down inside on the kick-boot bench against the wall, just behind the door, so that that was all you could see then, after my father had sat down, just one leg crossed over the other, showing out from behind the left-open door, my father's khakied legs, one leg lopped over a stood-up knee, with a tiny-to-see one-and-two toe-wag-around lazy, and his back-laced-around-the-top dirt boots looking to me like nothing that my father always said they were, a dirt-tired pair of old dogs.

Then I would be the man in the way, the last man alive for my aunt coming down, and then the first man to go and tell about it, to just go to the bedroom door to tell my sisters about the first part before the rest, when my sisters would have to come out and sit at the table and watch and listen to my aunt bend the branch her way as to how things were going to spring right back up to rights.

. . .

During the first part, which I could see through the porch-door window and hear the most of across the backyard, I could see my aunt doing the telling with the pointing to my father sitting down, with the "We'll see after," and the "Who'll smart after," that would always go with the pointing down at my father until it was finished, the first part, and I would go then to the downstairs refrigerator to get a cold can from the bottom row and bring my father out the beer he liked to drink before he had to get the dirt off, before he undid the back-laced-around laces and pulled off the dirt boots slow and then went over to the sink to scoop the sandy-clay soap out of the yellow can, with my aunt still talking and pointing, and the cold water running for sandy-clay soap that my father scooped out, big-thumbing the yellow can set into the wire rack, the sandy-clay soap he first gray-muddied-up his hands with, and then spread on up into the black swirly hair forest of each arm to a bone-naked elbow, the cold water running still, before making the sandy-clay mud-slide, mud-run, and mud-flood-away off, both arms held up under the faucet, like a boxer waiting for his gloves, when I would watch my aunt point a last, or next-to-last, straight-shook finger down toward my father's bent-over back, with a "Scrub hard, and look to where your dirt runs," and I would hear her wedge-heeled quick-walk back to the house, when I would just go stand then, outside under the fruit trees, while my father moved inside to close the door a little and to take off his khaki clothes, that I could only hear and not see come off, hear only the little clunk of the double-eye belt buckle part of, when my father would drop his khaki pants down onto the table inside, and I could hear then the little metal clunk sound that the thin steel made when my father stepped inside the put-up-portable shower that he and my uncle had put up to leave the dirt outside where dirt belonged, my aunt had always said, and I could hear the pull-across sound of the shower curtain and the turn on of the water sound you could make almost in your throat, when I would always know it was all right for me to go back just then into the washroom to sip the foam up out of the beer can bottom, and all right for me to go stand to just look at my father while the water was still running and the curtain was still pulled-across shut—my father, moving a little side to side behind the gray-white plastic clouded curtain, and me hearing then the splat sound of something flat to falling water and then the sound like rain makes on something tin and hollow, and then the clunk sounds of a someone, or it could have been a something, I thought, when a something-you-didn't-know-what was moving up over you on top of a tin roof, before my father would turn the handle wheels of the water off and I would run back into the house to get a clean set of top and bottoms and a pair of fist-rolled socks out of my father's bottom drawer and run back to put them up on top of the table in the washroom and then close the door behind good, while my father dried himself off with the green, rack-hung towel, alone in the washroom, and put on his home clothes up off from the nail board and swooshed, in his Father's Day-bought brown-leather slippers, across the backyard and in to dinner.

Then would come the sit-down part, when it would sometimes be just a finger length of twig down on an empty plate in front of a sister, and my aunt not even pointing, just talking about who had the smart answer now, asking if anyone had the smart answer to these things before dinner, and my father would say to let's just everybody eat now, without what-all commotion in anybody's ear until after the dinner, until after a man could sit down to a piece of bread for a minute without a tree falling down onto his plate that he had got himself clean to sit at without the commotion, and then my father would tell everybody to get their plate as well clean and to take, take some first.

During the passing and the spooning and the cutting and eating, I would put the little stick fingers passed under the table into my pocket, and my aunt would put the speckled blue roast pan or the two-ton iron stew pot in the middle of the table and say to let a hungry slave do the rest after this family, the rest after her ironing and folding and looking-all-after and letting her own husband wait upstairs like a field hand for his dinner, all for a bunch of wild hairs flung in her face, like a wild woman he and all here knew well of, my aunt would tell my father, for all the neighborhood to know that she, my aunt, was just a stood-up tree in her own house to be back-talked back to by a handful of skirt trying to be a dress under this one roof, and that he, my father, ought to have the at least half-pinch of decent brother's breath left in him to do the least some little thing about it, about this "come from a she-wolf, be like a she-wolf" everyday slap in the face without fear or shame in front of God or the postman.

Then my father would say that he would put the shoe on to fit right on this family after the dinner, after a man could have his dinner sit in his stomach for five minutes out of the day without every passing creature come to soil on it, any stray bit of dog on the street come to take his ease on the place where a man was taking his dinner after a day's work, if it was at all possible to a man not given to ask much of his God to have a goddamn moment to see where the rock was in the shoe and to be able to take care of it with a crumb's worth of peace and quiet over his table. And my father would get up out of his chair, with a "Don't everybody else get up," and go out back to walk under the fruit trees in the garden, while my aunt quick-walked up the iron-gated stairs with a loud bing sound ringing all over the house, and then my father would swoosh back in a little while later, when my sisters would be already scraping plates into the garbage in the pantry, and sit down at his place at the head of the table and eat quiet while my sisters soaped up the sink-stacked rest of the dishes, and I, each by each, dried up the silver.

·   ·   ·

When it was my father, alone in the dining-room alcove after dinner, sitting in his lion-paw-knuckled oak armchair at the table, listening to the news at the tiny-bulbed hand-me-down wood radio, leaning up close so that he could hear what my father said was the man's English, and me still in the kitchen doing my one-potato, two-potato with the spoons and the forks and the knives all to lay out even before I could close back the drawer, my sisters would do their stay-away from my father back on the back porch and put on a whisperlike other kind of record than the scratchy one that was the Combined Choirs of St. Vladimir's and St. Nikodim's that was my one favorite one to put on, and my sisters would sit down on the long pew bench against the wall or around the back round table with the lion claws cut deep into the wood legs at the bottom, and sew into their round-hoop wood things that my aunt would give them to stitch flowers in, and I would go into the dark pantry and take the stick fingers out of my pocket and put them all under the potato peelings and waxed cartons and tin cans in the garbage, and sometime around then, before the man with the news was all finished, I could hear my aunt quick-come down the stairs, the gate bing and then the music *pik-puk* stop.

Before the man with the news was all finished, the wind and the weather would start up, the commotion that started at the top of the stairs and came down onto the back porch and on into our rooms downstairs with a weather vane of its own, along the hall and into the front room where my father was listening close to the man's English—my aunt holding the pointiest-one-twig black finger, me watching from the doorway to the kitchen, my aunt holding the twig switch in one hand and then turning with a click and pulling off straight the little-screw-lost white knob of the wood radio, reaching over the table in front of my father, pulling the white knob off and then putting it into her front blue-button-up-sweater pocket with an "If you don't, then I will."

Then my aunt would throw the switch at my father's feet, then pick it up again and put the switch into a quiver, shaking and looking for what my aunt said was a one sorry among her many sorrows, a one sorry that my aunt said she could not find anywhere between the three of them, anywhere at all in a talk-back house that was going to stay her house and none of it other, and my sisters would first hold up their hoop things with the needles still hanging down from them, and then back up like a boxer would, I thought, yes-and-no back, yes-and-no back, all the way out of the hallway, with my aunt saying, "Sorry-yes!? Sorry-yes!?" every time down with the nubby end-quivering black finger, until I could see my father stand up and take off the double-eye belt, and then it was "Answer this!" and "Answer that!" and then just my sisters' arms up without any hoops and needles now, and my father's "Answer her something, just!" and all the things I could always hear when there was a commotion in the house: the flat sound of the double-eye belt against skin, the sprung-bump sound of dropped wood frames bent thin into circles and the sound of the switch against just skirt when it missed bare leg or arm—all the sounds of a commotion that brought my uncle, with always a couple-of-two-good-dollars' worth of change in his home-clothes gray pants, coming down the stairs with his late-to-church clump and bing and "What's the holler?"

What the holler was was something I should just listen to and know well what was good for me, my uncle from upstairs would tell me, telling me then to just keep back out of the way of things, when the way of things was not my business to put myself in front of, when the tree stood shaken and it was not my tree to shake. "What's the holler-crazy?!" my uncle from upstairs would say to the ones who were hollering still. "What's crazy about to high-holler in the house?!"

The holler in the house that my uncle said was crazy-odd lunatic to put in the ear of a neighbor, in the ear of the whole neighborhood, was just one more holler that I could hear on the back porch, the last back room where my sisters would go to get away from the black finger and the double-eye belt, in the corner by the porch window, where my big sister would pull down at the flap-down ironing board and stand huddled behind it with the other two sisters like a shaken sister-tree, what was half pulled down and half slid fallen out to a dead-end stop, flat to ceiling and floor, like the hard clap of the wing of the last-minute-always-there angel, who could wing down out of pure air anytime and put an angel wing through even a wall, my aunt would tell me, sharp and fast and hard as the quick of an arrow, without an arrow's afterward thin quick quiver, but hard down-falling as the wing bone of the Cross—what I thought from what I could see from behind the twist-iron gate and hear holler and screech of in my ears—my upstairs uncle doing the hollering now with the rest and grabbing at the flapping tongue of my father's double-eye belt, yelling at my sisters, "Don't raise your arms to my face! Show you to raise an arm where it don't belong!"

Then my uncle from upstairs would grab the twig switch from my aunt, because my father said the double-eye belt was but his godforsaken business to buckle up both any hell down here and his goddamn pants with, and then my uncle would say that he was going to show my sisters now what belonged and what did not under his roof, and my aunt would *pik-puk* put the needle back down onto the record and fumble the finger switch over to where it had to be for the wood stand-up Victrola to start to play, and I could hear my sisters crying still over the music that was for dancetime and dillydally, and I could see the wishing wells and buckets falling down around my youngest sister's red-looking legs with bumps all on them, until my biggest sister would push her hair back out of her face with the backs of both hands and look straight at my father and say, "You stop it!" without crying anymore that I could see, "You stop now!" just like that to my father, and my father would unroll his fist-wrapped-around double-eye belt and throw it like a snake into the corner by the porch door and say he would kill God out of anyone that touched it before he did, including my aunt and my uncle, and any man on God's earth that might come walking through that door to lay another hand down to his children, and then my big sister would push the flap-down ironing board back up and take my other two sisters, arm-wrapped-around past my aunt and my uncle from upstairs, on into the big-iron-bed back bedroom just off the porch, and close the door behind good, and then my uncle would scratch the needle off the record that my aunt always told us was for dancetime and dillydally, and my uncle would tell my aunt then to stop the goddamn thing going before he went and backed out the Buick and rode right the hell right over it, and then my father would walk out of the back-porch door, out under the fruit trees, with the yellow bug porch light flicked early to ON by my last-man-home-always upstairs uncle, the bulb already getting a few early pinch-wing moth moon walkers under the jut roof out over the door—my father, whom I could see under the trees staying his stay away from the light—me standing, last man in the doorway under the early, yellow-light-footing moon walkers, here and there a little winged moth moon-wink, and my aunt, moving behind me, flapping flat shut the wall door to the ironing board and dropping down, snap-button good, the wood cover to the stand-up Victrola, and my uncle binging the iron gate behind him going up, saying everybody could just go eighteen ways back to hell before he would soon bother about a damn bunch of high holler—my father, whom I could see moving under trees, with the inside bottoms of his fists raised up to his eyes, like a boxer covering up when it is all over and the referee has to step in, I thought, or maybe just even looking like the way it looked to me at church—my father looking to me then like the man who was Adam, my aunt would tell me, Adam in the high lead-vined colored-glass church window that I passed slowly by with my aunt on Sundays, going down the long aisle inside looking up at the black lightning of the lines in the cracked glass circle under the eaves—staring up always at the cracked man who was Adam, with his fists raised up to his eyes and no tears that you could see, crying down on one knee in the corner and covering up to the light where God was, high up over the trees of the garden, because God had given the woman in the picture, my aunt would tell me, the willow of hair to weep in.

The State

of California

My father and I sat on the
green bench, throwing peanuts out of the bag for the squirrels to come and crack, so that we could watch what my father
said were creatures smarter than we were watch us right back,
my father looking, every other peanut or so, at the green-
painted screen door of the nearest yellow building, where my
father said the woman I should never regret to call my mother
lived somewhere in a room inside, the two of us waiting for
the nurse to come and hold the door open and walk down the
woman I had only remembered seeing dressed in the cream-
white wedding dress in the wedding picture up over the bed,

walk the woman down the cement-block stoop and out onto the feathery-shadowed lane so that we could all have our nice visit.

What I saw when the green-painted screen door finally opened was a woman in a white dress, with white stockings on and white shoes and a white nurse's cap stuck down into her hair, walk down the stoop with her arm looped around another woman's arm at the waist, the other woman, wearing a print housedress like my aunt always wore at home and brown tie-up shoes, doing a little skip-dance step ahead of the woman in the white dress, and looking down at the path most of the time, as if she were looking for the right place to pick up her key or her jack, and hop the chalk-marked steps to the moon or to home free.

Even with whatever short cry or long-halled cry and metal-clink sound that I could hear from the yellow buildings that looked to me like the red-tiled-roof, creamy-stone-blocked main building of my school, with the same fence-wired screens on the lower windows that we had facing the playground to keep the stray-hit or odd-bounced, window-busting ball out, and even with the swishing sounds that the trees made whenever the breeze came up, I could hear the woman in the printed housedress counting one-two, one-two, and see the woman

doing a little skip-dance step as the two women walked toward my father and me, where we were waiting on the bench
under the small-moving, feathered shadows of light, with
their arms looped like square-dance partners, it looked to me,
or held like the way my father held my mother's arm around
his arm in the wedding picture hanging by the twisted wire
over the bed I slept in with my father, the two of them standing between the slanted-up tall white candles, fresh and unlit
for the picture, stuck into the stand on either side, with the
cream-white train of the dress splayed out see-through, like a
feathery-light, long gauze curtain, caught on something, it
looked to me, and stretched out thin as far as it could go
over the rose- and leaf-dappled carpet, with the veil draped
down into the long hip-wound swirl fanned out in front at the
bottom of the picture, the two of them standing together
like a pair of old-time skating partners stuck to this one spot
on the ice, the woman cape-and-long-scarf frozen to the pond.

I listened to the woman in the housedress counting until
my father put his arms around the woman and kissed her
on each cheek and smiled big, and then the woman in the
white dress said to my father that he had a nice-looking
nephew, and my father said then that no, I was the son, the
boy, his wife's boy and not any nephew, and then the woman
in the printed housedress looked at my father and said, "Who's
that?" and my father said to the woman in the white dress

that it was only because his wife was not used to seeing me, that she could only remember me little and was not used to seeing me big yet, and that he would get it all cleared up in a jiff-minute.

Then the woman in the white dress said for us to have a nice visit, and for the woman in the housedress, whom she called Charlotte, to have a nice visit with her family, and then walked the nyloned-buzzed steps back toward the yellow building, while the woman in the housedress did a little-girl show-off step in front of my father.

I watched the woman in the housedress do a heel-toe and heard the woman that my father called sweetheart count one-two when she would point a big-toe split seam of brown shoe down at the ground, while my father said that I was Eddie, just her little Eddie a bit grown-up, a bit bigger than she might have remembered, and for her to just take a look at little Eddie grown-up, little Eddie with his own-put part in his hair. Then the woman in the printed housedress with no belt going around through the string loops around the waist, and with the little tummy jiggly under the thin dress, turned the face toward me that I knew from the wedding picture over the bed, and sucked at her front teeth and at the spaces around them where some teeth were missing, looking a glinty-eyed squirrel-stare my way for a long time, I thought, while my father just smiled big with his arm around the woman's waist, pulling the woman in to him bent.

• • •

I sat on the bench next to my father while my father pulled the box of cherry chocolates for us all to eat out of the paper bag he had brought, and then pulled out the box with the new, same-kind of brown shoes in it for the woman who was my mother to put on, the same kind as the pair of split-seamed shoes that she did her heel-toe, one-two with when she was doing her little-girl dance for my father. "They're ugly," the woman in the housedress said.

I walked on my father's side of the trees, carrying the box of chocolates while my father carried the bag with the brown shoes in it under one arm and looped the other arm around the arm of the woman who was my mother, while the woman, from time to time, did a little two-step. My father said that it would be all just fine pretty soon, that we would all go dancing when the right time came, soon as he could find his cracked old dancing shoes to polish up twice.

I held the box open for the woman who was my mother, while the woman fit a big-toe-stuck-up foot with no nylon on it but just the bumpy skin into the new dark brown leather shoes, pulling up on the string slow. "But I already have these ones," the woman said, "these ugly ones."

When the woman in the white dress came out of the green-painted screen door again, my father said that it was time to say good-bye for now, that I had to get back home to go to school, and for the woman in the housedress to kiss me, Eddie, and to just stay on getting healthy until the doctor said what the best thing next was for everybody, until maybe things would all be all right the next time, when she could maybe come home for sure, home for a good long healthy visit, or maybe even home for good.

I stood up to get kissed and to kiss the woman who was my mother on the cheek when my father said it was time for a son to kiss his mother, and I took my father's hand first before I put my face up and looked at the woman looking back at me, at the white glinty dots in the woman's eyes that kept moving from side to side, like the squirrels' eyes did when they sat up and looked at you before eating the peanuts, looking all over everywhere at me except at the place where I was doing my looking, as if there was something behind me that I could not see, I thought, until my father told the woman to bend down so that I could reach, and then I could see the woman's shiny dark eyes glint a look somewhere past my look, at some place behind me, while I just looked then at the place of skin that I would have to kiss.

I waited on the bench under the row of trees while the woman in the white dress, wearing the skinny-lined-at-the-back, white buzzing nylons, put a hand at the shoulder of the woman who was my mother and hooked her arm and said, "I'll take her," to my father, and while my father walked just a little behind, all the feathered-light way to the yellow building, like a man still going on talking to the dancing partner who had been tapped on the shoulder away, it looked to me, my father saying, "Next time, we'll all go home together next time," for as long as I could hear under the high-swishing echoey trees, the two women quick-walking without ever stopping until they had gotten to the screen door, the woman in the printed housedress looking to me to be pulled away by her new partner, to dance this way or skate that way, pulled to go faster than she maybe wanted ever to go, over a slippery, sawdusted dance floor or across the ice.

I stayed by where the bench was and threw the rest of the peanuts as far as I could out onto the grass and watched the squirrels sit up and look first, before cracking the shells with their teeth or running the nut back up the crisscross-trunked palm trees and swishing up through the dry hanging part, stringing down under where the first green fronds peeled away from the bark and drooped down at the tips like an umbrella. And I just sat down with the shoe box with the old shoes in it next to me on the bench, and waited for my father to come out of the screen door in the yellow building at the end of the walk, the yellow building that I could not hear any sound come out of now, except the little sound like a tap when my father finally pushed the screen door out with an arm out stiff, putting his hat back on his head and letting the door shut back when he reached up to fix the brim.

I stood with my father, a shortcut-across-the-lawn while later, out on the curve part of the sidewalk, where the cars coming in along the row of pole-tall palm trees turned around the orange-flower-bedded and green-bush-planted long bar of curb-held dirt running down the center of the road, the curve part where the black-and-white sign was, stuck down in a block of cement by the curb of the sidewalk, that said TAXI STAND on it, so that I could just see the brown bear flapping, if I looked up to the top of the tower building with the red-tiled, pyramid roof, the brown bear on the white flag with his one red star, that my father said was the only thing left to claw down for any poor beast stuck that high up in the sky, the bear that looked to me as if he were dancing around the pole whenever the breeze blew up, and my father waved his hat at the Yellow Cab when he saw the car coming, and opened the door out so that I could get into the backseat first, and then my father told the taxi man wearing the yellow cap with the round part on the top poked out into sides and corners like an umbrella, the man who was listening to another voice now besides my father's, coming out of the black box hooked up under the chrome-grilled curve of the dashboard, the black box I could see the dark round hole of behind the square net stretched across the circle, the voice that was swishing on the S's and buzzing on the Z's, like some small clawed animal scratching on a screened porch door to be let in or let out, I thought, told the taxi man that we might just settle for the best way to the bus station of the town nearest, if the taxi man did not know of a good shortcut to the moon, and that he, my father, would give him every dollar in his pocket and a dime extra if the taxi man did, and then my father asked the taxi man if he knew a hotel in town with a dining room, not too many odd two-steps away from the bus station, where a tired old hoofer and his son could get themselves a dog-decent good meal and a moon-faced double-wax shine.

Snowland

When my mother was home-come to stay for the holidays, my aunt said that my mother would strangle us in the night while we were sleeping and that there was no telling what else my mother might do, not being used to what it was like being home, keeping a home for a man at work breaking his back, and not staring at a cup of coffee all day or at a fly on the wall or sitting down at the kitchen table blotting up toast crumbs with a wet-sucked finger, singing little bits of ditty songs to the linoleum, not used to taking any good care until she was told what to do and all how to do it, and that there was just no telling what a woman like that would do around a fuss of young girls and a boy rat-scared of the dark, who had to be walked the whole way to school, a little boy you would have to be wall-crawling crazy to forget you ever had, and just no telling what kind of a crazy package this crazy man, my father, had decided to dump on my aunt's doorstep in the middle of Christmas.

While my aunt was in the swing-door kitchen, showing things to the woman who my father said was home-come to see how she would like it, and to see what it was like to have to clean a stove and do the dishes when the dishes weren't yours, and how to cut up a loaf of French bread for a bunch who picked the white part out of the middle and dipped it in the mayonnaise jar when even you weren't looking, my youngest sister and I made Snowland under the tree, my youngest sister always getting to do the flaky-sprinkle houses how she wanted to do them, and getting to put the yellow-windowed church and the mirror pond where my sister said a yellow-windowed church and a mirror pond had to just be, according to Nature and not even according to her, and getting to stick the already-snowed-on little twisted-wire-and-fuzz green Christmas trees in the places where my sister said it would be Nature's spot to stick them, and putting down all the little red-and-white-candle choirboys where my sister said they would not look too giant big for the pink- and blue-windowed little houses and for the church with the steeple, out in the snow of Snowland, in some valley alone or stood together on a hill, where my sister said it had snowed already, and no more snow had to fall, and where it was not all that cold to sing out in because the little red-and-white-candle choirboys all had robes on, and where my sister said they were singing "Silent Night" only, because that was the right song to sing after a snowfall and because the candle choirboys all looked like the same boy anyway, me just getting to do the white plastic reindeer with the little red eyes and the little red dots for nostrils, the white bucks going after the mother deer and her baby at the mirror pond that was my aunt's looking-at-her-hair-bun mirror, and going after each other up on top of what we said were the mountains, the white plastic deer with just grooves for hair, stuck-antlered over who was going to be king around here, because we did not have any right-looking things for Wise Men or for a Joseph or for a Mary, or for any shepherds anywhere, and my sister said a marble in a half-opened matchbox was some crazy idiot's idea of how to sleep a Jesus.

Because we did not have what my youngest sister said was anything near right, anything close to a Joseph, and because my sister said I was dumber than the spool I brought to make Mary, my youngest sister said that we could at least make an angel. I did my deer race out over what we said was just the rest of Snowland, while we waited for my aunt to show my home-come mother how she did butter and mayonnaise and cut up bread for lunch, my deer race not anywhere even near the little village that we said was waiting for Christmas inside behind the pink and blue and yellow windows, but just in a place where we said that it had snowed already, and while my youngest sister cut out white paper wings and pinned the pieces onto the back of one of the little choirboys with straight pins from my aunt's sewing box, saying that it was close enough for an angel, waiting on a mountaintop for Joseph and Mary and for all of the Wise Men and the shepherds that we did not have anything just right-enough-looking for, waiting for them to come to that flat place that looked to me just like any other snowed-on place good to deer race on in the anywhere of Snowland, waiting for them to come to what my youngest sister said was the only right place in this Nature to put down Bethlehem.

While I was doing my deer race over the places flat enough and far enough away from anything special, or doing my deer fight over who was going to be king of Snowland, and while my youngest sister pulled the Venetian blinds shut to plug in and test the lights on the Christmas tree to see how they would look over all the hills and valleys of wrapped-around sheet and over the mirror of the pond, my middle sister came out of the swing door of the kitchen, letting out the sounds of what I could hear to be the voices of my aunt and my home-come mother and my oldest sister, all yelling different at the same time, and what my middle sister said to my youngest sister was for her to come into the kitchen quick to help my aunt get the bread knife back, and what my middle sister said to me was to stay good away and to run out of the screen door if my home-come mother came out of the kitchen alone.

I stayed on my side of the swing door, in the room that was darker now for Snowland, where I could see the lights of the Christmas tree in different colors in the glass doors of the china cabinet against the dining-room wall by the swing door, and where I could hear my aunt's voice in the kitchen saying, "We don't need this now, do we? We don't need to cut no more bread!" I stayed on my side of the swing door with a pulled-out dining-room chair for in between me and whoever would come out, until it was just my youngest sister who pushed the door out, handing me the wire-square flyswatter and saying I could use the flyswatter to keep the bigger woman from hitting my aunt and knocking my aunt's glasses onto the kitchen floor, for only because my aunt had taken the knife away.

I pushed through the kitchen door behind my sister and what I saw was the woman who was my home-come mother with her back up against the sink and her arms held up in front of her face, slapping back at my other sisters, the sister with the twig switch hitting and the other sister just slapping with her hands at the elbows and arms of the big woman at the sink, while my aunt just hit sideways at the woman's shins with the flat head of the broom and yelled at the woman to smite her, my aunt, before the woman should smite these, her own.

I took my turn to hit with my flyswatter at the woman at the sink who looked to me bigger than my aunt and bigger than any of my sisters, until the woman stopped hitting back and let a few switch hits on her arms just make her eyes blink for a moment, so that the woman could look right down at me holding the wire-square flyswatter and say, "Don't hit me. Don't hit me, Eddie."

I waited outside in front of the house, where my sisters said I should play on the sidewalk or on the lawn and stay out of people's driveways until my father came home. I rolled my little black-rubber-wheeled orange delivery truck with the chipped back tire on the sidewalk and down the hill of the neighbor's driveway into the black-tar gutter that was the dump, the little orange lead truck with the pretend man in the front who you had to say was driving the truck because it only came with the windows empty and did not look like any-thing near what I said it was when the truck rolled over on its back, so that you could see the gray underneath, when it would look like just a piece of hollowed-out lead with holes cut out in places and would not look like a man, stopping to make deliv-eries or racing to the hospital in an ambulance, or just stopped

halfway down to the dump to fix a tire, and I could see the
lights, still shining in colors through the blinked-open lines of
the Venetian blinds, get their brighter blue and red and green
and orange, it looked to me, in the early dinner-dark, when I
could see my father walking from where he came down the
long roll of sidewalk from the top of the hill, his knees knocking a knob into the big loose overalls that my father always
wore to work, with the little black gorilla head on the copper-
colored, shoulder-strap-hook buttons, and wearing his overall
jacket with the big gray gloves flapping out of the side pocket,
and his striped cap that I said had to make him be the engineer
that my father never said he was, but only said that he was the
man who oiled the wheels, my father, whom I could see from
the long block away, swinging his black lunch bucket, until
my father was close enough for a good long roll of what he
bent down and sent zooming my way on the sidewalk and
then into the grass gutter, smiling big when I picked it up:
the blue plastic wagon-car with yellow wheels on it that my
father said was good for a load of anything he could think of
that minute in the whole world, the thing my father zoomed
at me on the sidewalk before I could stop it rolling or before
I could see what it even was in the early dinner-dark, and that
my father said he found in some ditch at the rail yard and
brought me home early for Christmas, before I could remember to say that the woman my father had left that morning
drinking coffee in the kitchen, was aunt-swept and locked up

behind the red-ribbon-bow-tied, cut-glass-doorknobbed door
of the bedroom.

When the puffy red-faced and raspy-scare-voiced doctor came,
I watched with my sisters from the dark wood hallway looking into the bedroom, where I could see my father holding the
arms of the woman who was my mother, crossed down on the
bed over her lap so that the woman could not get up from the
bed, and holding his face close enough to the woman's face
to kiss the woman if my father had wanted to, I thought, while
the doctor pinched the skin up on the woman's arm in a place
or two before the doctor found the right spot to put the needle
in, and I could hear the woman, while the doctor was holding
the cotton on, say over and over that my father was acting all
crazy again, that it was too early then for anybody to go to
sleep at all.

When the men from the white truck came up the porch
and in through the screen door, my father said for my aunt to
help him to sit the sleeping woman up and to get her a button-
up sweater pulled on because it might get cold on her later,
before I could see the men from the white truck wrap a white
blanket thing around the woman who was only just home-
come for Christmas, and pull at the sides getting it snug, and
then go back and forth out of the bedroom and into the hallway so that they could get the bed thing straight through the

door, my sisters and I moving out of the way into the front room and watching through the door into the hall, and my aunt holding the screen door open for the two men from outside on the porch, and I could see the eyelashes of the woman just flutter as if she was only pretending to be asleep, I thought, as if the woman could wake up any minute and say that it was too early for any kind of bed, flutter that I could see up close when the woman wrapped up in the blanket thing was big in the skinny hall with the two men from the white truck, and then big going out through the doorway, the woman who looked to me then to be dreaming, looking at things move in the dream behind her eyelids, the way I dreamed about rats all the time chasing me and woke up and had to sleep the rest of the night with the light on, looking to me then, from where I could still see from the porch, like someone who had fallen asleep outside when it had snowed all night and had been covered up by the falling snow, with just the eyelashes twitching as if there was something caught in her eyes under the eyelids that the woman could not wake up enough to reach a hand up out of the heavy-fallen blanket of snow and just blot out with a wet-sucked finger, and looking to me to be somehow warm under the red-blinking light on top of the white truck, before the men wearing white pants and white jackets put the woman where my aunt said was the best place now for her and for everybody, in her own little room behind a door where there was peace and quiet and not a whole family to have to keep and wash white and not fear to smite in the dark out of some coffee-jittered-up, knife-raising black dream.

I watched the red light of the white truck blink the long blocks down the street, the white box with the night-empty windowed doors darker and then lighter under the hung-over street lights, until the white truck turned away at the red, yellow and green-dotted signal light onto the big-store street at the far corner, and then I hopped the porch steps back inside to have a last night look at Snowland and a last sister-stopped wagon-car zoom under the dining-room table and to put maybe just two of the white fighters down to the mirror pond to drink, while my aunt made coffee in the lit-up kitchen for her and for my father, and while my sisters put on pajamas and pulled the covers back to sleep the night with the light left on, me taking a long night look at the colored tree lights shining off the glass doors of the china cabinet and shining in the cut-glass diamond of the doorknob of the door swung into the front room from the dark wood hallway, and then just looking at the colored lights all over Snowland and at the place that my youngest sister said was the only right place in this Nature to put down Bethlehem, and then taking one of the little red-and-white-robed candle choirboys, one stuck in just a valley where we said it had snowed already, and then wrapping around the red-and-white-robed candle choirboy with a black wax dot for a mouth open, with a clean white, folded Kleenex from the box in the bathroom, and putting the boy with the white-waxed stubby wick coming out of his head down in the blue plastic wagon-car with the yellow wheels on it that was the biggest thing then in Snowland, bigger even than the pond, but closer-looking, I thought, than just a marble in a box, down to sleep under whatever light in this tree of heaven anyone else looking might choose to call his star.

Listening to Jesus

During the long, do-
nothing summers, when my out-of-the-coal-mine, into-the-
wine-barrel youngest uncle, as my aunt would always call
him, would tell my aunt and Jesus-to-Christ-listening that he
was flat-damned and all-too-alone crazy watching the grapes
turn black all day on the farm, with the Mexicans looking at
him like he was a scarecrow on the property and not any kind
of man who belonged to the property, tending to good purpose on it, but just stuck there to draw yellow jackets and to
trap gophers all day long and play gin rummy to nobody else
in the kitchen all night only, because he had not two lousy

cents and a dime to go the half-mile down the road to the Injun Hut to get himself even a draw of what piss water they got off the tap, like any other white man walking on the surface of the earth with something to do partnered up to other hands human, and not to just the goddamn gopher he was going to catch, by Christ Heavenly, who was even starting to look down his nose at him, down his nose and then only going back in at the last minute anymore, as if even the gopher knew what even a scarecrow looked like, and that leaving him out there to be dogged to by a dumb dog in front of every passing picker was not the right way, by Christ Jesus, to treat a man who was of the same blood as my aunt and my father, running there in any blue vein he could point to on his still-good-for-something arms, besides just to be a stick-stuck empty shirt in the wind without not the two cents and a dime in his pocket to sit among men for half an hour before going back to a house black with night, without not even sound inside of it except the dog nails on the linoleum and a short leg of log burning up in the stove just for the sound of it burning or to heat up some all-week-old mulligan stew that he could not anymore look at by himself, my all-too-alone-crazy youngest uncle would say—during the long of those summers when there was a farm still for us to go to, my out-of-the-coal-mine, into-the-wine-barrel uncle would sometimes stumble up the driveway back in the city, a day or two days stray before the sometime Saturday when we would all go out to the farm together—stumble up to the back-porch door with his hands in his pockets, saying right to me or to my aunt, who would always come down from upstairs, or to one of my sisters, or just to the things he would look at hard, that he was no good to Jesus anymore for it, not at night like that anymore out there alone, without not two cents and a dime to jiggle in his pocket in a place where more than just his two feet and a dog's stood together—no good to Man-my-God-to-Jesus anymore for it, and that he would rather tap out a few mayonnaise jars or pickle jugs of red to a passing Mexican so he could give the money to the bus driver and ride the bus in like a man with a still-good-for-a-pick-and-shovel couple of arms and legs on him—ride in and not have to walk the sixty-odd miles like a beggar to see his blood own, face to face around a table, before the sometimes all-together-skipped-over-forgotten odd Saturday when nobody would care to remember that he was even out there like a shirt stuck on a haystack, with a dumb dog to feed, always breaking the chain every week whenever a yellow jacket got under his tail, and that he would rather tap the red in his veins all day and all night for just the bus money, before he would ever leave that black house to tramp down to the Injun Hut at night with whatever vat-soaked money he could get and let a rag-on-a-scarecrow pickled-up Mexican buy him a wrist jerk or a long arm of what piss water they had got pissed out that night for the "Peace-to-what-ails-you."

Then my aunt would ask my all-too-alone-crazy uncle if he had fed the dog, if he had remembered to open a can for the dog, and my uncle would never be able to remember who ate the week-old rest of the mulligan, he or the dog, or if he had paint-stick poked out a half-can for the dog or not out into the cast-iron fry pan by the doghouse where the yellow jackets were, or if even he had remembered to lock up the back-porch door to the house out there for certain, and my aunt would say to my out-of-the-coal-mine uncle that he had his head in the barrel again, that he was a man walking around with his head in a barrel that my father or my other uncle—her good husband, next-as-close-to-blood own—would bust open with a hammer from the garage if they caught sight of him come in no account stray to home, leaving the sheep to the wolf, just to wet his cork local to home and neighbor, leaving a dumb dog tied up to die on the line and wine smell all sweated-out wet under his armpits to a stink still all over on him for just anyone to smell besides only herself, and that he had but short of one half hour to eat a salami-and-cheese sandwich sit-down, before he had to get right back up on that bus and go back like the Good Shepherd who would not ever desert us, and that he could have me to take along for the company, if that would put the cork on him, to play his goddamn-always gin rummy with, if that was the ticket, and to take twenty dollars to pocket—her run-out nylon own money—to get at least a bag of flapjack flour and canned milk and some kibble for the dog if it was not yet dead, and an Eskimo Pie for me, the boy, to hold things over until they, the rest, got there to put the tin lid back on things, the next tomorrow or the tomorrow after that, depending on what day stray it was that time, and my aunt would tell my out-of-the-coal-mine uncle then to take his wine-soaked shirt off for her to wash with all the rest, and to put on a clean, same-size work shirt of her husband's and a clean undershirt too, and to do it all in three specks less to the half hour, by her clock counting, and I would sit down then with my uncle and eat a baby skinned potato out of the blue roaster or a ladle of lentil soup or pink bean soup with blubber-thick pieces of home bacon in it to just leave in the bowl, or maybe just a fat piece of hard-to-get-the-scalp-off salami and the little kind of pickles that my aunt always put with it that took what my aunt said was only a little speck second to put on a plate, and then my aunt would go to get me gum for my pocket out of her purse in the bedroom drawer and I would take the box that had the big black ace of spades on it out from the scissors-and-string drawer in the kitchen and put it in my button-up sweater pocket, and my out-of-the-coal-mine uncle would say then that I was a crook, that I had eyes in my head already crooked to crook him on the bus, and my aunt would tell my all-too-alone-crazy uncle to crank up his lip and drink down the water she put for him and get going to wait for the next bus coming before her good husband or my father came home and put wheels to his barrel and rode his wine-soaked head over every last bump in hell.

Before anyone could come to put wheels to his barrel, my uncle and I would take a paper bag of apples for the bus and run-walk down the cement driveway to the sidewalk, where I would go out past the yard-long redwood fence first to see if just maybe there was a Buick turning this way by the corner light or if my father was maybe turning that same two-blocks-to-walk big street corner, walking under the always-lit-up, pink-glowing sign that said COCKTAILS in tubed neon writing under a skinny-up-to-the-V-topped glass with a supposed-to-be-neon cherry sitting down in the V-bottom of it, and if there wasn't any Buick or just my father coming, so that we might have to go out the backyard good-neighbor gate and walk across the good-neighbor flagstone-set-in lawn and down the good neighbor's driveway to take that side street, my youngest uncle and I would take then the always-best shortcut to the big-store street, the long of those summers when my uncle was a day or two stray and all-too-alone-crazy come back to know exactly what day it was or what barrel he was supposed to be in, my youngest uncle would tell me, but just only knew where, by Christ, the big bus stopped that was going our way, going to the place where my uncle said the fancy buses were too high-toned to go, the ones that did not stop just in front of Five and Dime anywhere like this one did, where he said he knew just the where it stopped, just the nickel-and-dime good-for-nothing place where the big old Peerless would clunk open a front wing door like a chicken does its wing, I thought, and take even jack-anybody in if he could come up with the ante, my uncle would say, in, right in front of nickel-and-dime here and dump him jack-out-of-the-barrel into piss-water nowhere—us

146

running-walking the short way to go, through the gravelly
back of the doughnut shop parking lot, where my father coming home or my other, next-as-close-as-blood-own uncle, driving home in the Buick, was not so likely to walk or drive
through—us running-walking to catch the big one different in
the distance from the other yellow-and-green all-the-time-
running city buses, the ones that ran past the Hagstrom's and
the bakery and the toggery where we always got socks and
handkerchiefs for my father, with the no-headed suit-men stuck
on pole stands in the window—us waiting for the speck of
minutes left in front of the red-signed Five and Dime for the
big, cut-corner-front-windowed bus to come and get us and to
stop for certain like my youngest uncle said he knew it would
stop, and open out the door slow, to me and to my out-of-
the-coal-mine uncle—the different-opening, nothing-to-see
through, big metal door that we would have to walk way out
away from the curb to stand out in front of, the door closed up
tight, and then stand back away from for the door to make the
cranking sound starting, and then the metal-wing pulled-back
clunk sound that the door made when the metal wing-bone
lever flat-locked to open, like the sound that my other uncle
made when he hammer- and chisel-hunked the metal rings
down around the wine barrels to make them tight, I thought—
me clunking up the rubbered steps of the bus then, and my uncle clunking up behind, reaching, as I waited, for the money
that my aunt had given to him to pocket, and pinching the one
bill that I could see was a twenty into a long, bent-over V-shape

147

to give to the bus driver, while the driver pulled in the stick-up handle and the wing door closed back shut, and I would chicken-walk toward the back first, crooked along the narrow aisle, high with big brown seats and what I could see of people, here and there, sitting in them, and my uncle would stumble behind, holding on to the soft brown tops of seats by people's heads sometimes, with a half-fistful of bills in one hand and two skinny brown tickets stuffed into the half-fisted other hand—me crooked down to my shoes in the going bus, crooked as a spare jack, cut-corner bent in a little on the one-eyed and on the two-eyed ones that I liked always to grab up no matter what, whenever we played gin rummy or jacks or better—me crooked from my eyeballs down to my chicken-split feet, my uncle would say, looking for a pair of empties so I could climb up in and be by the window and see all as much of the where-we-were-going-to before it would get to be dark, when my uncle would turn on the baby bulb light under the metal rack over our heads that sent a cone-shaped tower of light, small to big, down to the itchy-fuzz brown bus seats, where my uncle would snap down his no-good-to-a-hill-of-beans spades or sometimes turn over his good-enough-to-win pair of kings—the light that was like a real beacon, I thought, and not like the little soft spread of moon glow around the top of the tiny plastic lighthouse, plugged into the wall of the bedroom, that my aunt would turn on at night so that I could go to sleep in the rest of the dark—and my uncle would say that he did not care whoever won the game so long as nobody crooked him, so long as he knew the when-to-get-off-the-barrel and the crooked damn bus driver, crooked for taking a damn straight three dollars for just a chicken-split kid, knew anyway the goddamn-where-he-was-going-to, knew the place the way my uncle said he knew places in the world, the ones he had crawled out of like a scarecrow, black as night, when there was not any more day left behind ever, and I would feel the big bus bump over the road as we played gin rummy and sometimes even jacks or better where the light was small on the itchy-fuzz brown seat, when I could not see anymore exactly the where-we-were-going-to through the round-cornered window of things in the dark, and my out-of-the-coal-mine uncle would say then that he was sick of pulling no-good-to-himself-a-damn clubs or hearts or whatever would be no good to him to pull that game, tired of me pulling always the jack on him, and Jesus-to-jack-Christ tired of looking at my crooked face crooking him black, and that he was good for only Paso Robles, fold or no can open, and that if I had eyes to tell an Indian from a two-pump gas station, then I could go ahead and pull the yellow string down for the bus driver to stop, to go ahead and stop and drop us crooked jacks in front of the Injun Hut, near the black-as-night, grape-grown-around farmhouse where God's gopher had crooked him back into the hole—Paso Robles, fold and no can open, sonny, bust as a scarecrow in another man's shirt, my out-of-the-coal-mine uncle would say, and for me to go ahead and pull the yellow string down if he were to unlikely fall asleep, or even if he were still awake then, to go ahead and pull the string when I saw a pink Indian with a feather and a log cabin crouched underneath, pull the string down for the crooked bus driver to stop this goddamn barrel going and to let us out, my uncle said, out to gravel over to that good Indian's hut to see what piss water they got pissed out that night, scarecrow special, and that he had a few stiff feathers left in his pocket to give to the good Indian to go ahead and crook him good, the way God had already crooked him black, and take his easy lid right off, like foam swiped off the top of a glass of piss water, and then my out-of-the-coal-mine uncle would reach into his pocket and give me a couple of flapjack dollars for the store in the morning, saying that he but probably did have some mulligan left enough for us and the dog, and for certain, bacon hung up on the nail, and my uncle would give me the two quarters I liked to give over to the red-and-black-checkered-shirt man with the mustache like Buffalo Bill, who was the bartender—the two quarters it took to get the Eskimo Pie that the red-and-black-checkered-shirt Buffalo Bill man kept down in a black-topped freeze box next to the ice cube bin with the dewy-necked, grip-capped bottles I could just see, sticking up out of the cubes, and a quarter extra to play cowboy songs with on the red-and-blue-lit-up jukebox, and then my out-of-the-coal-mine uncle would reach up and turn off the baby bulb light and say it was no use anyhow to crawl out of any hole that God held up high the lid to and that even a dumb gopher knew that, and I would shuffle back the cards together in the high-seat dark and look to see if the line was still good on the bent corners of the jacks by the just-enough-changing-light of the window, and I would put the box of cards back into my pocket and take an apple from the paper bag to hold me over, and bite a tooth window into the skin and pull a strip off and just hold the piece in my mouth for a while, thin, like the skin scalp of an apple, and roll it around on my tongue for just looking long out of the window, and I would look out then at dark set-in places under trees that passed by and at the dime- to nickel- to quarter- to bowl-size-big lights, with hunkered-down cars pushing the round head-lights out toward us, it looked to me, the last car coming along dimmer just behind the rest—one or another hunkered-down car caught in the beams of the barreling bus for however many bus-blinded seconds, with the light, slant on some part of wind-shield face showing out from under a hunkered-down, pushing-up-closer car roof, that I could see from the high-up-barreling-bus window, before it would go back to dark, before the car would push past the double beam of bus lights and cut, with a shiny fender stuck forward, back into the dark, the windshield face or faces passing us dark-sided by, and I would look out slant to the window for as far as I could see ahead around the fuzzy brown seat in front, for the place set in from the other side of the road where there would be ice cream on a stick and a high, shiny, red-topped, spin-around stool for me to spin around on, with a slow chicken-walk under high, big trees home to the bump-nose-stung, chain-choked-up dog always afterward, and sometimes even a boost-up crawl through the side bathroom top-pulled-down window when the back-porch door would be uncle-locked, like my all-too-alone-crazy uncle would say then that he had known damn well all along that it had been locked, except for the jackass key that he had jackass left in his button-up shirt pocket so as not to forget it, and that he was just a jackass scarecrow in another man's shirt, my out-of-the-coal-mine uncle would say, those times when he would forget the key in a shirt pocket or when my aunt would find the key later, left on the dresser in the city, when I would be the one to have to go up and over, good like a gopher, into the no-sound tiled bathroom and be the only sound in the house then that I could hear, me gopher-quick going through the shade-pulled-down bedroom, with my uncle walking around on the rock-grinding rain gravel outside of the house, saying loud to me, that I could hear through the walls and the windows, that he was not gone anywhere away, but still was right there, and that nothing was going to get me, and saying for me not to worry about any dumb kind of dark so long as he was still kicking, and I would get to the kitchen part of the house then, where it was lighter through the shade-pulled-down, lemon tree-shadowed windows because of the moon in the yard, but where the kitchen linoleum sounded all different, crinkling out to the corners, as if there were somebody or something else on it besides just me that I could hear moving, maybe over by the stove, I would yell out to my uncle between steps, or moving in the front bedroom, which I could only maybe see the dresser-by-the-wall part of and not see the anybody who could be behind the closet door, pulled out open, so that I could only see a dark door space that maybe a man was deeper back inside of instead, and my out-of-the-coal-mine uncle would grind the gravel over to a kitchen window and stand close in front of the window for me to see what my uncle said was only him, for me to see a man shape, bigger and smaller, moving in front of the window with the shade pulled down, and to hear the voice of my uncle saying for me to just go ahead across the linoleum to the tiny back room, where there were only a couple of dumb cans of dog food up on a shelf, and some bacon strung up on a nail, and not any man who could be standing there in the little room —to just go on over all the linoleum quick and to turn the pinch lock on the doorknob so he could come on in and flick on the light to show me that there was not another soul there, and to go ahead and do it then, like a good boy, good as a gopher, and not to listen to what was just the dark talking, but only just to him, like I would listen if it was Jesus talking, standing right there in the window where I could see him, big as a scarecrow, with nothing else out there except his two feet and the dog's—me looking slant out of the round-cornered bus window those times during the long, do-nothing summers when my all-too-alone-crazy uncle would fall asleep with his mouth a little open on the itchy-fuzz brown bus seat, saying some words that I could hardly much make out to be able to say afterward what he had said exactly, except to be able to tell my uncle, shoulder-jiggled awake in the high-seat dark, that I had heard him talking like a scarecrow—me looking out then for a pale pink feather of light, stem-stuck into a curving band, hunkered hollow around a high-as-a-chimney nickel Indian's pink-glass headful of barrel-deep dark.

The Gathering

The summer on the farm
when my sisters crawled down under the vines to clear a long
dirt path out away from the white farmhouse to the wild apple
tree on the down-the-hill corner of our property, that grew
small, green-spotted apples too sour to eat, picking away the
little porcupine-spiked brambles that blew off of the weed
grass that grew under the muscled vines and the grapes, saying
that the wild tree was going to be our separate house and that
we would keep the path rock-and-sticker clean, like a smooth
dirt carpet, so that my aunt would let me take off my high tops

and walk out barefoot like my sisters, what my aunt said was ankle-naked like an Indian, the whole way out across the vineyard, without the tied-up firm support to the arch that the man at the shoe store had told my aunt was his flat-out recommendation—the summer we hands-and-knees cleared the long dirt path out to the wild twist of tree that my aunt said God had wasted on a vineyard, when the Mexicans had already picked the vines clean for the barrel, and when it was that time with stone fruit when the farmers said you either had to eat it all up off the table or dry it in the sun, or cook it up and put it in a jar, the people from San Francisco drove down for a Sunday with their loop-handled shopping bags and orange-mesh sacks and cardboard boxes to help themselves to whatever heft of sweet fruit my aunt said they could carry back to San Francisco in that high-toned new car, fruit that would be more than a bird could swallow and less than what my aunt would need to boil up with a couple of pounds of sugar to keep a four-kid family eating their right jarful of God's promised bounty all the hard-raining winter through to peach-blossom spring.

I sat up in the wild apple tree barefoot lookout while my sisters picked the little spiked dry stickers off of the dirt path and made ridges on both sides of the path with their hands smoothing the dirt, picking out the bigger rocks and throwing them off to the side, lookout saddled over a branch while my uncle

156

took the people from San Francisco tree to tree and vine to vine around the property, the little man in the polished black shoes and the short-sleeved shirt with the little umbrellas on it, and the big woman in the polka-dot dress and the white wedge-heeled, open-toed shoes, and the man who the big woman said was their special houseguest back in San Francisco, the white-skinned man with no eyebrows and no hair anywhere on his head that you could see except for the no-colored eyelashes, the bald-all-over man in the light-colored pants and the see-through rippled thin shirt, reaching up with his white, hairless arms and pulling down the sun-blackened figs, or the apricots or the peaches low enough on the branches to reach, pulling down and rolling the black fig or the ball of pit-stoned fruit in his hands every once in a while before putting the piece of fruit into the loop-handled brown paper bag that the big woman's husband held up for the big woman and for the bald-all-over man, the little man going from one to the other under some tree until the bag was filled up, when they would all stop and wait for the little man in the city-straw hat and the shirt with the little umbrellas on it to run-walk back to the cement patio under the big shade tree out back of the white farmhouse, and put the full bag down on top of the picnic table, and then step back into the hot sun out over the big dirt clods, trying to keep his polished shoes from sinking into the softer dirt, I thought, shouting, "I've got one right here! I've got the empty one right here!"

. . .

I sat up barefoot lookout, with my black high tops back at the porch stoop, lined up with my sisters' shoes, barefoot Indian so that we could live at the apple tree house the way that the Indians had lived on the land before it was ever a vineyard, the Indians of Old California, whose arrowheads we sometimes found in the dirt clods after the plowing, Indian teeth skinning a sour apple and looking down at the weed-picked and broom-swept space under the tree, and down at my sisters, bent over in places along the dirt path, picking out the rocks and throwing them out under the vines and pinching off the stickers that were everywhere in the dirt, me on the lookout for my aunt, making tuna lunch in the green bowl back in the kitchen for the people from San Francisco, and on the lookout for my uncle, going down the hard, dirt-divided length of the property to the highway, and then along the small, hill-humped-across width, both white- and red-grape-planted in rows, bringing the little man with the short-sleeved shirt with the umbrellas on it, and the big woman in the polka-dot dress, and the man in the light-colored pants with no hair anywhere on his head, row by row closer, stopping to cut a big V-shaped cluster of the white grapes still on the vine that we only cut to keep fresh on the table or to fill a crate for a neighbor, my uncle stopping sometimes instead to cut whatever small cluster of red grapes he could find that the Mexican pickers had missed, and that we had stacked up fresh picked in boxes in the garage, ready for crushing in the big, one-ton vat, my uncle cutting with his hook knife and putting the cluster into the orange-mesh sack that the big woman held up, or into the loop-handled brown paper bag that the little man held up, until my uncle and the people from San Francisco walked into the apple-tree clearing that we said was our house like the Indians had and that you could only go into barefoot, and then the bald-all-over man reached up for what my uncle said was good only for birds and Mexicans and not a bite destined for any white man, and pulled off one of the small hard apples and rolled it around in his hands and then wiped the apple off with a white handkerchief from his pocket before taking a small dirt-destined bite.

Then I saw the bald-all-over man look for a place to put the apple and the little man said for him to just drop it into the bag that he held out, and I watched my uncle take the tooth-scalped apple then and throw it out into the vineyard, saying that this earth could always use another worm to help with the plowing. Then the bald-all-over man said that he was thirsty, that the sour apple had made him thirsty and could someone get him a glass of water, and my uncle said then that he would send the Indian if the Indian was not too crippled to walk back to the house to get a guest a drink.

I slid down the nubby bark and walked slow over the path that my sisters said was smooth as a carpet now, while my sisters just stood around under the apple tree picking stick-ers off of their shorts or making the little walls of rocks straighter around the place that they had swept clean with the yard broom, walked slow over the rocks and the stickers that were still scattered along the path the long way back to the house, stopping to brush the little round porcupine balls from between my toes or to just stand on a smooth place for a moment and watch the weed hoppers jump onto the path and then jump back off, making a cricket sound, me walking by myself then without my sisters to hold on to when it hurt, walking and sometimes having to crawl hands-and-knees down when the ground got too hot for the bottoms of my feet, until I got to the cement patio under the shade tree, when I could walk like a boy again and not have to walk like an Indian, crossing the mountains and the valleys and the deserts of Old California ankle-naked in the dirt, walk right up the cement stoop and onto the cold linoleum to get a man with no protection, it looked to me, with nothing between him and the sun except that white skin, a glass of clear water that we tapped cold from the spring.

The man said it was dirty. The bald-all-over man said the glass that I had carried over the mountains and the deserts and the valleys was smudged and asked if I could go back to the house and get him a clean glass, some other glass where the water would not look so cloudy and the glass so smudged when he held it up to the sun, and my uncle said for me to race like an Indian right back to the house to get the man a clean glass from my aunt before the man died of thirst, before a man not used to the best climate God could wrap around a grape melted on his property right out there in the sun.

Then the little man in the city-straw hat said that maybe it was time to go in now anyway, that maybe they could pick a few more figs and take a look at a pomegranate or two around by the house, that maybe the lunch was ready anyway and that it was a good time to take a little rest, but the bald-all-over man said that he would like to stay for a while longer in the sun, that he did not get much of a chance to be in the sun where he came from, and that he would be happier to join them later, after he had gotten a little more sun on his face, if only someone would be kind enough to bring him a little chair so that he could sit out by the apple tree and not have to come in just yet, a little chair that he could just put down on this smooth part, the bald-all-over man said, and, oh yes! a clean glass of water.

I walked over the mountains and the valleys and the deserts while my sisters and my uncle and my aunt and the little man in the city-straw hat and the umbrella shirt, and the big woman in the polka-dot dress all sat around the picnic table out under the shade tree, walked like just a boy in my hot canvas high tops that my aunt said would keep any crippled wooden Indians out of her house for good, with a boiled-clean mason jar full of tap water and a wooden folding chair that my aunt kept in the closet for when we had company extra for dinner, over the dirt path to where the bald-all-over man was just walking around the space we had cleared, wearing the kind of dark glasses that clip on and then flap down over a regular pair, walking around the lines of rocks that we had squared on the ground and called walls, like a man whose house had been struck by lightning or burned down by the Indians while he had been gone, I thought, walking around as if he were looking for the places where the door and the windows might have been so that he could build a new house, with the wild tree right inside of it, and start all over again.

I held the jar while the bald-all-over man folded out the chair just where the path went into the vines, and then I gave the man the mason jar that the man held up to the sun before sitting down, saying all that he had wanted was a glass of water and not the whole well, and then the bald-all-over man reached into his pocket and handed me a quarter out of his change and put the rest back into his pants, and said, "Thank you," and that he would be in in a little while, for me to tell the others that he would be in when he was ripe enough and to leave him just a little something to peck at when he came back.

My sisters and I carried the loop-handled paper bags, two kids to a bag, to the new car parked in the gravel driveway, the paper and the orange-mesh bags full of peaches and apricots and plums and the cardboard boxes full of white and a few red grapes, and the smaller boxes of black figs cleared off the table and heaped around the shade tree so that my aunt could spread the lunch—carried the bags out to the open-doored and open-trunked new car that the little man was packing, the new car that had the molded red plastic Mohawk man stuck in the chrome strip on the hood, while my aunt cleared the picnic table of the green bowl and the jar of pickles and the bowl of black-pitted olives, and twisted closed the long family-size loaf of sliced bread, leaving a white square of tuna sandwich on a paper plate with a paper napkin spread over the top and a fork sat on top of the napkin, all to keep the flies off, while the big woman in the red-polka-dot-print dress walked under the fig tree closest, looking up for maybe just the one or two fat ones that it was a shame to waste on the birds, I heard the big woman say, a big human shame.

When my aunt had cleared the paper plates and the napkins and had done the couple of forks and spoons and knives and a few bowls in the sink, and was out in the garden with the big woman in the polka-dot dress, walking with the big woman around the lemon tree and the pomegranate bush, and holding up her apron to catch up the fruit that the woman was plucking down, and while my uncle was in the garage showing the little man the one-ton vat full of grapes that had gone through the hand-cranked, V-shaped crusher, the stemmy pulp waiting to be forked out into the smaller, open-slatted wine press, my sisters and I watched the bald-all-over, red-as-an-Indian man eat the tuna sandwich that had been left on the picnic table and drink red wine from the gallon jug out of the wide-mouth mason jar, us looking through the slit under the shoved-up, cloudy-glass bathroom window at the bald man sitting all by himself at the picnic table, while we stood in the bathtub and scrubbed the dirt off of our feet, passing back and forth to each other the scratchy wooden bristle brush, scrubbed off what my aunt said was the dirt of twenty Mexicans, so that we could show the people from San Francisco how the Indians put out the fire in the house.

I did it without my high tops, I did it ankle-naked like an Indian, and sometimes I just stood in the middle like a wooden Indian that my sisters danced all around, but mostly I stomped around in a circle, holding onto my sisters' shoulders, saying that the tepee was on fire and that the ground was red hot, hotter than fire and hotter than the sun, and hotter than the Devil-down-below, while the little man in the city-straw hat and the umbrella shirt reached into his pocket, and while the big woman reached into the little black snap purse in her white, over-the-shoulder strapped bag, and the red-as-an-Indian, bald-all-over man with the dark round glasses still flapped down reached into his pocket also and flipped up the coins into the big dark, seed-, stem-, juice- and skin-filled vat—the nickels and dimes and quarters that we reached down and picked up out of the squishy slush and held tight in our

purply stained hands—the big dark, iron-banded vat that we
said was Old California all on fire, all the mountains and the
deserts and the valleys and all the houses of the Indians, on
fire in the White Devil's pot, shouting down that we were the
last Indians that Old California had left, the last four Indians
in the last burning-down house, in the last valley before there
was the great wide water, doing the last Indian dance that went
hot-foot, cold-foot around in a brother-and-sister skin-splitting
stomp, me watching my sisters' legs so that we could all do
the squat part together, me trying to rush the beat and say it
the loudest:

>Putting-out-the-fire, putting-out-the-fire!
>Sitting-on-the-flame, sitting-on-the-flame!

Constantinople

On the Saturday night before church the next morning, and the welcome dinner afterward for the king who they said had had to flee his country because of the war, and who had come to San Francisco to visit his people, before the welcome dinner when I would have to say my poem on the stage for the man whom I had only seen in pictures, dressed up in the blue, gold-braided uniform, with his hair all combed back straight, my uncle said that he would not mind taking me and my father and my aunt on a little run over the bridge to San Francisco, on the other side of the bay, to the house of a fellow countryman who was having a few people over to toast the crown and to get the blood of the Serb going again, saying as well that I could use the extra practice standing up in front of a friendly bunch, and that he had gassed up the Buick good to get us there and back easy over the long high bridge that tunneled through the island mountain stuck in the middle of the water between our smaller, darker-at-night city and the city of tall buildings and lights twinkling across the bay on the last hills of land standing before ocean, the city with the green-domed building lit up at night that I said looked like a palace whenever we drove past, coming down off of the bridge into the city or turning up the ramp to go back home to where it looked so much flatter on the other side, the shadowy-towered bridge with the yellow lights goosenecked out over the double yellow lines striped down the middle of the roadway, and with the long tubes of steel pipe that sloped down like ropes between the tall bolted towers, the twisted steel cables, looking to me always ready to snap like stiff suspenders, looped tight under the down-hanging swoop of curved-up pipe, and saying that it was a nice night for a little run in the Buick over all that black-as-aces water that I liked to stare down at out of the car windows, rippling in the sheen under a moon and lapping up only a dirty green under the bright white lights of the big ships floating in harbor between the long gray port buildings fingered out into the water on our side of the bay, and saying that I could ride up in the

front seat, as usual, between him and my aunt, and that my father could sit in back with his hat, and that it was a good time
to try out my new blue double-breasted suit that my father said
was what a young man going to see a king should sport, a good
time to dress up as if we were going to church so that he and
my father and a few friends could drink down a drop together
for what was lost and what was won, and for king and country, and so that I could put a few boy wrinkles into what my
aunt said made me look like the President, a good time to practice my poem that I would have to know cold for the next day
that my father said was going to be a flag day for Serbian boys
and for any true Serb with blood still in him, when they would
pass out the little blue-and-white-and-red-striped flags of Yu-
goslavia that they always passed out to put in your lapel to
show that you had bought a ticket to the church dinner, a last
chance to practice in front of people what I had learned with
the tutor, saying it over and over again around the house the
whole month long, the poem that my father and the tutor and
an old friend of my father's had sat down and remembered out
loud between them, about Mukhtar Pasha and the clod of
earth from Montenegro, about how Mukhtar Pasha had run
all the way back to the Sultan Murad with the dark clod of
earth tucked under his tunic, and had fallen down then onto
his knees in shame, begging the great Sultan Murad not to cut
off his worthless, three-times-bobbing-to-the-floor, Turk-turbaned and battle-bruised head.

. . .

Gliding over the bridge, I watched the cables rise up and get taller as we came closer to going under the high, X-crossed beams of the shadowy towers rising up into the fog, the towers that my uncle said held up the bridge like shoulders held up suspenders, watched the cables rise up and get small again, sloping down to the roadway, and I listened to cowboy songs on the radio, with the little light glowing under the glass-windowed notched band of numbers on the dashboard, listened the whole way across the water except when the car passed through the tunnel in the rocky island mountain that we called The Tomb, when the voice went dead on the radio until you came out alive on the other side of the big mound in the water, when the faraway twinkling lights at the arc end of the bridge bunched up into signs and buildings and cars moving, the fog-clouded mound in the distance looking to me like a big toy city, with churches and palaces and towers and tall toy men lit up bright to guard the city, like the big neon soldier boy with a round clock for a chest and for a stomach propped up on one of the buildings that you could see just ahead, gliding down away from the bridge towers, getting bigger and bigger as you got closer, and the tall sign with the white-bearded and white-turbaned old man in the yellow robe, holding a neon cup to his mouth, propped up on top of the building to one side of the bridge where it smelled always like coffee, with one sandaled heel raised up behind him, as if the old man was stepping out to meet the cup that he was holding to his lips, it looked to me, stepping off of the roof with the next step because the man was not looking anywhere down where he was going, the way I was looking from the high roadway gliding down off of the bridge, looking out at the high blue-and-red-striped tower with the lit-up number seven and the lit-up number six on it, and at the smudgy white face of the clock notched with X's, I's and V's on the tower of the paper company right off the ramp of the bridge that looked to me like a pointy-roofed parapet of a castle or a palace, and looking at the bright white neon sign out over a cluster of dark buildings that glowed JESUS SAVES through the mist over the city, me looking down out of the windows of the black Buick as the big car glided away from the water toward the lights that rolled up into the hills as if we were on a magic carpet, I thought, gliding over the city, and thinking that all the buildings out there were like things asleep in the dark, humps under the night listening to the same cowboy that I was, just humps sleeping out under the stars, while the neon soldier boy with a clock for a chest and for a stomach, and the tower with the lit-up number seven and the lit-up number six, and the sign with the old man in the yellow robe drinking from the cup, looked to me to be watching over all the dark shapes while the cowboy was singing, the neon soldier boy ticking all night awake and watching while my uncle looked for the right hill and then the right street, and while my uncle reached over and turned off the radio and clunked down the safety brake in front of one of the all-next-together houses on one of those hills and said then that it was time for every Turk to get out and walk the rest of the way to Mecca, walk up on his own sleepy-numb pair of pilgrim legs.

At the top of the arched stoop, I watched the tall man in the brown suit with the skinny white stripes, watched him walk down the inside stairs of the house, me looking through the looped-metal-leaf and vine-grated glass front door, and then we all stepped in, following the man inside and up the stairs and down the hallway to the place that the man said was his little wing in this big white bird of a house, big enough for his little flock, the man saying for us to just come right in and join the others who had had their glasses filled already at least twice, the men dressed in suits sitting around in the front room and the women dressed in silky dark dresses with polka dots or plain-colored dresses with cloth-covered buttons, the kind of dresses I would see in church, the man saying for us to come on in and make ourselves at home and to have a little glass of something to put some Serb blood back into our veins.

I watched the man fill a glass for my father and one for my uncle from the round-shaped bottle on the mantel, and I took one of the toothpicked pieces of ham rolled around a little pickle that a woman who came out of the kitchen started to pass around the room on a plate, and I looked at all of the pictures hanging on the wall by the mantel, the old black-and-white framed photographs of people standing together in groups wearing what looked to me like costumes, people with staring faces standing or sitting down on chairs up on a stage, and I stared back at the picture with the beautiful woman who looked like a Christmas-tree angel, standing in the middle behind a row of men all sat down in chairs, except for the man in the feathered helmet standing at the end, men dressed up in what looked like shiny white, baggy-armed shirts, some wearing uniforms with swords hanging down from belts crisscrossed over their shoulders, the whole group up on some kind of stage, it looked to me, with the beautiful long-haired woman, dressed in a silky-looking white gown, holding out the sides of the dress with her arms all stretched out, the silky white cloth making the wings of a butterfly or of an angel, I thought, and a man sitting down near me on a chrome-tubed chair from the kitchen, a man with a shiny gold tooth, holding a little shot glass, said that the woman in the picture was the *vila*, the fairy princess, the one who always comes at the end to save the play.

I took a skinny, waffle-sided cream cookie off of the plate that a woman was holding out to me and I heard my father tell the tall man in the brown, skinny-white-lined suit that he knew a little Mukhtar who was going to raise a few flags at the dinner to make them all proud when he said his poem, and I heard the man say that he was good for five U.S. dollars if that little Turk turned out to be a Montenegrin. Then I watched the tall, long-haired girl in the silky black dress that showed her bare white skin on top and the shape of her big breasts moving under the thin dress, carry a tray of coffee glasses with little handles on them out of the kitchen and put the tray down on the dining-room table by the shiny silver coffeepot and then go up and get a big hug from the man who said he was the father of the Angel of Grace, the angel who was going to save us all but only make one lucky man happy, the man said, the big girl I had seen at church once, standing with the man in the brown suit and with the woman passing the cookies, the girl that the men and the ladies were all clapping and laughing about, making the big girl with the red lips hide her head, laughing, in her father's shoulder, the men raising up their glasses and drinking, and the man with the gold tooth saying, "Brava, Milenka!" and "*Vila*, our *vila!*" slapping his hand on his legs and spilling his drink onto his pants.

Then the man in the brown suit with the skinny white lines in it said that all he needed now was a prince to go with his princess, and I could hear some of the ladies sitting around the dining-room table shouting out, "Brava! Brava, sweetheart!" and hear the man with the gold tooth, slapping his leg still and stamping his foot, saying, "Mi-len-ka! Mi-len-ka!" over and over while the big girl in the silky black dress held up both arms to the ceiling, and I watched the man in the brown suit pour out more of what was in the round-shaped bottle to the men who held out their glasses, the men saying to each other and to the man and to the laughing girl, "Long live our *vila!*" and "Long live the king!"

My father stood up then and said that he had the right

173

Turk for the job, a man with a little something to say to every-
one, and then my father took me up to shake the hand of the
big girl in the black dress and to tell the girl my name, and
then the man in the brown suit with the skinny white lines in
it said it was a good time now for everybody to get quiet so
that we could all hear what the Turk had to say that the man
said he thought would put the crown back where it belonged
the next afternoon, the crown it was going to cost him all of
five U.S. dollars to put right back onto the king's head.

I stood under the archway by the front door, where my
father told me to stand, watching the big white-skinned girl
with the red on her lips, the girl sitting in the windowsill in
front of the lights of the city, and watching the man in the
brown suit standing next to the girl with a hand on the girl's
shoulder, and watching all of the other people watch me,
standing up with little shot glasses or sitting around the dining-room table taking a spoonful of sugar or a dribble of cream
and then tinkling the little spoon in the little coffee glasses,
and I said the words that I had learned with the tutor, the poem
about how Mukhtar Pasha had begged the sultan not to cut
off his worthless head because he had not hushed up King
Nikola, and had not burned down all of the Montenegrin
houses at Cetinje, and because he, Mukhtar, had lost his whole
army and come back with only a single clod of Montenegrin
earth to offer up instead, and about how the sultan had jumped
up and backed away from the thing the sultan said was seeth-
ing fire and growing before his very eyes, when Mukhtar

Pasha had thrown the clod of earth at the sultan's feet, the
sultan calling for his servants then to throw the clod of earth
into the sea, the roiling sea, and about how the crier had had
to go through the whole city of Constantinople shouting out
that the Sultan Murad had gone mad and that the new sultan
now was Sultan Hamid, me holding my hands cupped around
my mouth and tilting my chin up, the way my father had
shown me, like a Turk at a bazaar, my father had said, like a
dry-throated Turk trying to sell his mother's old carpet.

After I had let my hands fall down slowly to my sides the
way my father and the tutor had said for me to let my hands
fall, my hands of the crier spreading the news throughout all
Constantinople, and while the people in the room were clapping and saying, "Bravo, Mukhtar!" and "Long live the king!"
the man with the gold tooth stood up and said that I should
get a kiss now from the *vila*, that every hero always got a kiss
from the *vila* at the end of the play, and then the man in the
brown suit with the skinny white lines in it said he had five
U.S. dollars for the hero who had the courage to go into the
other room and take the kiss he thought he deserved, and then
the big girl in the thin black dress with the shiny red on her
lips walked across the room and took me by the hand and
walked us through all the people sitting around the dining-
room table, and sitting on the stuffed chairs and on the sofa,
and sitting on the shiny tube chairs that had been brought out
of the kitchen, the man with the gold tooth saying that he had
spilled what courage it took all over his pants, me walking

175

behind the big girl in the thin black dress, watching the curved mounds of her hips move like the back of a horse on parade, I thought, all down the dark hallway to the room where somebody slept, where all of the coats of all of the people in the front room lay sprawled out on the bed.

I could hear the flat clang of the bell and the metal grinding sound of the streetcar outside the windows as the big girl knelt down and said for me to kiss her on the lips, to go ahead and just kiss her there where it was red so that we could just go out then and show them all the mark, so that everything would all be all right then, and so that I could get the five dollars, that all I had to do was to just put my lips out so that she could give me a nice red mark to show all the men out there where I had been, the color of what a nice friendly kiss looked like, just the red.

I stood and looked at the coats on the bed, at my aunt's coat with the fur going around the collar, laid up on top of a stack of other coats, and I looked to see if I could see my father's coat and my uncle's coat under the rest, and then I said I thought that the people could see what we were doing, and that the coats on the bed looked to me as if they could hear, as if all of the people were lying down together on a bed of snow with their arms held out like snow angels, looking at us. I said it was the streetcar. I said it was the light. I said it was my aunt looking at me from the pile on the bed.

I could hear the sound of the grinding streetcar and feel

the sound shudder through the boards under my feet as I watched the big girl stand up then, the big girl with the white-skinned breasts showing out of the top of her black dress with the skinny black strings going over the shoulders, and while I watched the big girl reach into a drawer of the dresser on the wall between the windows and pull out a tube of lipstick, and then look into the mirror of the dresser at where her lips were, and then at me, standing back by the bed, the streetcar grinding away, clanging the bell, as the girl pulled out the lipstick and rubbed the smooth red end around her lips so that they looked shiny, and then the streetcar only faintly a rumble as the big girl put the tube back inside, closing the drawer back with a little shove from her hips. Then the big girl took me by the hand again and pulled me into the closet, where I could see other coats and jackets and dresses close together on hangers, like people standing in a line waiting to watch us by the pull-chain light, I thought, the arms hanging down empty, and then the big girl knelt down again so that I could see down the front of her dress, and said not to worry about the five dollars, that everything would all be all right, that it was just us in the closet and that the other people were busy in the other room, that the other people had forgotten all about us, and that all I had to do was to stand still for a little minute that nobody else would ever see, not God, my aunt or even the king, stand still and just let the *vila* brush my cheek in the dark.

. . .

In the front room, while my aunt was wiping the red mark off of my face with a Kleenex out of her purse, and while the big girl wrapped her arms around her father in a hug, I listened to the men clink glasses and whisper to each other and then laugh, the man with the gold tooth saying that he would go next if he could run home and get his sword first, and then my aunt said that it was all right for me to just go do it, to walk across the room to where the big girl had sat down on the windowsill again with the lights of the city twinkling behind her, with the man who was her father standing next to her with his hand resting again on her shoulder, and then the big girl slipped off the windowsill and knelt down again so I could reach, while the men and the ladies shouted, "Brava, *vila!*" or "Long live the king!"—knelt down so that I could reach in between for the green bill folded up in the V of the rounded tops of the jiggly breasts that were showing over the black silky dress, reach in and then put the green folded bill into my pocket, while the ladies clapped or made clinking sounds with their forks against their plates, or with the little spoons against the coffee glasses, and then I walked into the kitchen with the woman who had been passing out the rolled ham and the pickles and who said she had a big piece of cake saved for me special, and a glass of milk, a piece of cake fit for a prince, the woman said, a prince who was going to show the king, the next tomorrow, how to wear the crown.

. . .

After I had crawled into my place in the front seat of the black Buick, and after my father had slid into the seat in back and pulled the door in shut, I reached and turned on the white knob of the radio while my uncle let the safety brake go and then honked the horn at the man in the brown suit with the skinny white stripes, standing and waving under the arch of the stoop, and I listened to cowboy songs on the radio as we rolled down and up and over the hills of dark houses, and as we rolled onto the ramp of the bridge that curved by the green, lit-up dome that I said looked like a palace, and I turned around so that I could kneel on the front seat and look out of the back window and see the soldier boy with a clock for a chest and for a stomach and the blue-and-red tower with the lit-up seven and the lit-up six, and the lights of the Ferry Building glowing in the fog down by the water, and at the lit-up sign with the white-bearded old man in the yellow robe, walking through the mist, it looked to me, stepping backward through the tall, rising cables of the bridge as we drove up the arc out over the water, the old man moving backward until he had to stop, with his back heel still raised up, and just drink what he had, I thought, stop walking like a sleepwalker over the roofs of some strange city, looking like a man who had walked all the way from Baghdad or from Constantinople, a sleepwalker who looked to me, looking back through the windows of the gliding car, as if he was listening to the same song that I was, and then I turned around in my seat and turned off the knob of the radio to see if I could still do it, say it all in front of just my father, sitting alone in the backseat with his hat, and say it in front of the sultan out there, looking up at the gray sea of night sky, say it whole before the big Buick rolled into the tunnel of the dark island that was a mountain in the middle of the bay, say it as if a sultan or a king were listening, or as if only God could hear, and I looked out of the back window, past the dark face of my father, at the toy city of lights, humped and glowing under the gray rolling magic carpet of mist, and I said the words all in my head, only in my worthless, Turk-turbaned head, the words of the poem that my father had picked out special with the tutor, saying the words for as long as I could, looking back at the man in the neon sign who I said looked to me as if he could be a sultan listening, or maybe just some other man, just some ordinary Turk looking for Mecca, the white-bearded old man holding the light-rimmed cup up to his lips and drinking up what my father said was the never-ending nectar pouring out over all the fog-glowing city, over the shadowy, red-light-topped towers of the bridge, and over the last hills before black ocean, the never-ending nectar pouring down through the twisted steel cables and floating across the roadway, me saying the words all in my head in front of God, my father and the sultan, I thought, before the big black Buick rolled under the glowing arched lip of the yellow-lit tunnel where the radio voices went dead, rolled into the tomb of the tree-shadowed mountain before I could finish crying out all of the news, the nectar pouring down over what my father said was all this dark hunk of earth flung out into the middle of nowhere, and as thick now as the bottom of that old Turk's cup, misting down over all of that dreamer's Constantinople like sleep, down out of his crazy Allah's tumbled bowl of night and stars.

A NOTE ABOUT THE AUTHOR

TED PEJOVICH has had a career in the theater—opera,
acting, dance. After service in the Vietnam period, he
performed in repertory, on television, and on Broadway.
He lives in Manhattan with his wife, actress Anne Mc-
Intosh, and their newly born son, Christopher.

A NOTE ON THE TYPE

The text of this book was set on the Linotype in Garamond No. 3, a modern rendering of the type first cut by
Claude Garamond (c. 1480–1561). Garamond was a
pupil of Geoffroy Tory and is believed to have based
his letters on the Venetian models, although he intro-
duced a number of important differences, and it is to him
we owe the letter which we know as "old style." He gave
to his letters a certain elegance and a feeling of movement
that won for their creator an immediate reputation and
the patronage of Francis I of France.

Composed by Heritage Printers, Inc.,
Charlotte, North Carolina

Printed and bound by Fairfield Graphics,
Fairfield, Pennsylvania

Designed by Julie Duquet